# Real-Time Phoenix: Building Scalable Elixir Applications with Live Updates and WebSocket Streams

Sam Stevenson

Published by Northwood Lore Books, 2024.

REAL-TIME PHOENIX: BUILDING SCALABLE ELIXIR APPLICATIONS WITH LIVE UPDATES AND WEBSOCKET STREAMS

**First edition. November 18, 2024.**



ISBN: 979-8230293217

Written by Sam Stevenson.

# Table of Contents

# 1. Introduction to Real-Time Web Applications

Real-time web applications have revolutionized how users interact with the internet, transforming static pages into dynamic, interactive experiences that respond instantly to user actions and server-side events. In today's digital landscape, users expect immediate feedback and live updates, whether they're collaborating on documents, monitoring IoT devices, or engaging in real-time chat conversations. This fundamental shift in user expectations has made real-time functionality not just a luxury but a necessity for modern web applications.

The traditional request-response cycle, where clients periodically poll servers for updates, has given way to more sophisticated approaches using WebSocket connections and server-sent events. These technologies enable persistent, bidirectional communication channels between clients and servers, allowing for instant data transmission and updates without the overhead of repeated HTTP requests. Elixir and Phoenix have emerged as powerful tools in this space, offering developers a robust platform for building scalable, real-time applications that can handle millions of concurrent connections with remarkable efficiency.

Elixir's foundation on the Erlang virtual machine (BEAM) provides inherent advantages for real-time applications. The BEAM was originally designed for telecommunications systems that required high availability, fault tolerance, and the ability to handle massive numbers of concurrent connections. These same characteristics make it ideal for modern real-time web applications. Elixir builds upon this foundation, adding a more approachable syntax and powerful abstractions while maintaining the battle-tested reliability of Erlang.

Phoenix, the web framework built on Elixir, takes these capabilities even further by providing sophisticated real-time features out of the box. Phoenix Channels offer a powerful abstraction for handling WebSocket connections, while Phoenix LiveView introduces a groundbreaking approach to building interactive web applications without writing significant JavaScript code. These tools allow developers to create responsive, real-time experiences while maintaining the simplicity and maintainability of server-rendered applications.

The advantages of building real-time applications with Elixir and Phoenix extend beyond just technical capabilities. The ecosystem promotes functional programming principles that lead to more predictable and maintainable code. Pattern matching, immutability, and the actor model provide elegant solutions to common challenges in concurrent systems. The supervision tree pattern, inherited from OTP (Open Telecom Platform), ensures that applications can recover gracefully from failures, making them more resilient in production environments.

Understanding the architecture of real-time applications is crucial for building systems that scale effectively. Unlike traditional web applications, real-time systems must maintain state across multiple connections while ensuring consistency and handling network issues gracefully. This requires careful consideration of state management, message passing patterns, and eventual consistency models. The Elixir ecosystem provides tools and patterns for addressing these challenges, from simple PubSub mechanisms to sophisticated distributed systems capabilities.

Security considerations take on new dimensions in real-time applications. WebSocket connections must be properly authenticated and authorized, and systems need protection against common attack vectors like connection flooding and message spam. Rate limiting and throttling become essential components of any production system, requiring careful implementation to balance protection against abuse with legitimate high-traffic scenarios.

Performance optimization in real-time applications involves understanding and managing various resources, from memory usage to network bandwidth. The BEAM provides excellent tools for monitoring and optimizing application performance, but developers must understand how to use these tools effectively. This includes managing process lifecycles, implementing appropriate garbage collection strategies, and optimizing message passing patterns.

One of the most significant challenges in real-time applications is handling scale. As user numbers grow, systems must efficiently manage increasing numbers of concurrent connections while maintaining low latency and high availability. Elixir's actor model and the BEAM's distributed capabilities provide powerful tools for horizontal scaling, but implementing these features requires understanding of distributed systems concepts and careful architectural planning.

Database interactions present unique challenges in real-time applications. Traditional CRUD operations must be adapted to support real-time updates and notifications. This often involves implementing event sourcing patterns, using change data capture (CDC), or adopting specialized real-time databases. Caching strategies become crucial for maintaining performance under load, requiring careful consideration of consistency requirements and update patterns.

Testing real-time applications requires approaches that go beyond traditional request-response testing. Developers need to verify WebSocket connection handling, test real-time update scenarios, and ensure system behavior under various network conditions. Load testing becomes particularly important, as real-time systems often behave differently under high concurrency than during normal operation.

Deployment and operations of real-time applications present their own set of challenges. Systems must be deployed with zero downtime, handle connection migration during updates, and maintain state consistency across distributed nodes. Modern container orchestration platforms like Kubernetes provide powerful tools for managing distributed systems, but require careful configuration to work effectively with BEAM-based applications.

As we progress through this book, we'll explore these concepts in detail, providing practical examples and best practices for building robust, scalable real-time applications with Elixir and Phoenix. We'll start with fundamental concepts and gradually build up to advanced topics in distributed systems and production deployment. By the end, you'll have a comprehensive understanding of how to architect, build, and maintain real-time applications that can scale to millions of users.

The journey ahead will cover not just the technical aspects of building real-time applications, but also the architectural patterns and operational practices that ensure success in production environments. Whether you're building a chat application, a real-time dashboard, or an IoT monitoring system, the principles and practices we'll explore will provide a solid foundation for your real-time application development journey.

# 2. Setting Up Your Elixir and Phoenix Environment

Before diving into Phoenix development, it's essential to set up a proper development environment that will support efficient Elixir and Phoenix application development. A well-configured environment ensures smooth development workflow and helps avoid common pitfalls that developers might encounter during their journey with these technologies.

Let's start with installing Elixir. Elixir runs on the Erlang virtual machine, so we'll need to install both Erlang and Elixir. For macOS users, the simplest approach is using Homebrew. You can install both with the commands brew install erlang followed by brew install elixir. Linux users can typically use their distribution's package manager, though it's important to note that some distributions might not have the latest versions available. Windows users can download the installers directly from the Erlang and Elixir websites, or use Windows Subsystem for Linux (WSL) for a more Unix-like development experience.

After installing Elixir, verify the installation by opening a terminal and running elixir—version. You should see output indicating the installed version. Similarly, check the Erlang installation with erl -version. It's crucial to ensure you're using compatible versions of Erlang and Elixir, as certain Elixir versions require specific Erlang versions.

Next, we'll need to install Phoenix. Phoenix is distributed as a Mix archive, which is Elixir's built-in build tool. Install it by running mix archive.install hex phx_new. This command downloads and installs the latest Phoenix project generator. You might need to install Hex (Elixir's package manager) first if you haven't already, which can be done with mix local.hex.

A proper development environment for Phoenix applications requires a few additional dependencies. First, you'll need Node.js installed for compiling static assets. Download and install it from the official Node.js website or use your system's package manager. Phoenix uses Node.js and npm (Node Package Manager) for managing frontend dependencies and compiling JavaScript and CSS files.

PostgreSQL is the recommended database for Phoenix applications, though it's not strictly required if you're building an application that doesn't need a database. Install PostgreSQL using your system's package manager or download it from the official website. Make sure the PostgreSQL server is running and you can create databases with your user account.

For code editing, while any text editor will work, using an editor with good Elixir support will significantly improve your development experience. Visual Studio Code with the ElixirLS extension provides excellent support for Elixir development, including features like syntax highlighting, code completion, and inline documentation. Other popular choices include Sublime Text with the Elixir package, Atom with language-elixir, or Vim with appropriate plugins.

Setting up Git for version control is also important. While not strictly required for Phoenix development, version control is essential for any serious development work. Install Git from your system's package manager or download it from the official Git website. Configure your Git installation with your name and email using git config—global user.name "Your Name" and git config—global user.email "your.email@example.com".

To improve your development workflow, consider installing iex-mix in your shell configuration. This tool provides enhanced features for IEx (Interactive Elixir), including command history and better line editing capabilities. For Bash users, you can add eval "$(iex-mix init)" to your .bashrc file.

Once you have all the basic tools installed, it's time to create your first Phoenix project to verify everything is working correctly. Open a terminal and run mix phx.new hello_phoenix. This command generates a new Phoenix application with all the default options. When prompted to install dependencies, answer "Y". The generator will create a new directory containing your Phoenix application with all necessary files and directory structure.

After the project is generated, navigate into the project directory and configure the database connection. Open config/dev.exs and adjust the database configuration according to your PostgreSQL setup. Typically, you'll need to modify the username and password fields to match your local PostgreSQL installation.

Create and migrate the database by running mix ecto.create followed by mix ecto.migrate. If these commands complete successfully, your database configuration is working correctly. Finally, start the Phoenix server with mix phx.server and visit http://localhost:4000 in your web browser. You should see the default Phoenix welcome page.

For development convenience, set up some aliases in your shell configuration. Common aliases might include mps for mix phx.server, mpr for mix phx.routes, and iex -S mix phx.server for starting an interactive Elixir shell with your Phoenix application loaded.

Consider installing additional development tools like Phoenix LiveReload (included by default in new Phoenix projects) which automatically refreshes your browser when you make changes to your code. The ExUnit test framework comes built into Elixir, but you might want to add additional testing tools like ExMachina for factory creation or Wallaby for integration testing.

To make debugging easier, install the Phoenix debugger by adding {:phoenix_live_debug, "~> 0.1.0"} to your mix.exs file's dependencies. This provides an interactive debugging interface in your browser during development.

For working with Phoenix channels and real-time features, ensure your system's WebSocket capabilities are working correctly. Modern browsers support WebSockets natively, but if you're planning to develop behind a proxy or in a corporate environment, verify that WebSocket connections are allowed through your network configuration.

Finally, consider setting up your development environment with Docker. While not required, Docker can help ensure consistency across development machines and make it easier to manage services like PostgreSQL. Create a docker-compose.yml file that defines your development services and use docker-compose up to start them.

Remember to regularly update your Elixir, Erlang, and Phoenix installations to get the latest features and security updates. However, be careful about updating production applications, as new versions might introduce breaking changes. Always read the changelog and test thoroughly before upgrading production systems.

With your development environment properly configured, you're ready to start building real-time Phoenix applications. The next chapters will guide you through creating increasingly sophisticated features, but having a solid foundation with your development tools will make the journey much smoother.

# 3. Understanding WebSocket Fundamentals

WebSocket technology represents a fundamental shift in how web applications communicate, moving away from the traditional request-response cycle to enable true bidirectional communication between clients and servers. Unlike HTTP, which requires clients to initiate all communication, WebSockets maintain a persistent connection that allows both servers and clients to send messages at any time.

At its core, a WebSocket connection begins with a special HTTP request called the WebSocket handshake. The client initiates this handshake by sending an HTTP request with specific headers indicating its desire to upgrade the connection to WebSocket protocol. The Upgrade header is set to "websocket" and the Connection header to "Upgrade". Additionally, the client sends a Sec-WebSocket-Key header containing a base64-encoded random value.

When the server receives this upgrade request, it responds with a 101 Switching Protocols status code, along with corresponding Upgrade and Connection headers. Crucially, the server must also include a Sec-WebSocket-Accept header containing a specially calculated value based on the client's Sec-WebSocket-Key. This handshake process helps ensure both parties are truly implementing the WebSocket protocol and provides a basic level of security against unauthorized connections.

Once the handshake is complete, the HTTP connection is upgraded to a WebSocket connection, and the protocol switches from HTTP to WS (or WSS for secure connections). At this point, both client and server can send messages in either direction without the overhead of HTTP headers. The connection remains open until either party decides to close it, or until network conditions force a disconnection.

WebSocket messages are framed in a specific format that includes control frames and data frames. Control frames handle protocol-level operations like connection maintenance and closing the connection, while data frames carry the actual application messages. Each frame includes a small header that indicates the type of frame, the length of the payload, and whether the payload is masked.

One important aspect of WebSockets is message masking. To prevent cache poisoning attacks, all messages sent from clients to servers must be masked using a random key. This masking is handled automatically by browser implementations, but it's important to understand when building custom clients. Server-to-client messages are not masked, as servers are considered trusted entities.

WebSockets support both text and binary message formats. Text messages are typically used for JSON or other string-based data formats, while binary messages can efficiently transmit files, compressed data, or custom binary protocols. The choice between text and binary formats depends on your application's needs and the type of data being transmitted.

Connection management is a crucial aspect of WebSocket implementations. Unlike HTTP connections that are short-lived, WebSocket connections persist and consume server resources. Implementing proper connection lifecycle management is essential for building scalable applications. This includes handling connection timeouts, implementing heartbeat mechanisms to detect stale connections, and gracefully handling reconnection attempts.

Error handling in WebSocket applications requires careful consideration. Network interruptions can occur at any time, and both clients and servers need to handle these gracefully. Common approaches include implementing exponential backoff for reconnection attempts, maintaining message queues for unsent messages during disconnections, and providing feedback to users about connection status.

Security considerations for WebSockets differ somewhat from traditional HTTP applications. While WebSockets can use TLS encryption just like HTTPS (using the WSS protocol), they require additional security measures. Cross-Origin Resource Sharing (CORS) rules apply to the initial handshake, but once the connection is established, the same-origin policy no longer applies. This means applications need to implement their own authentication and authorization mechanisms for WebSocket connections.

Performance optimization for WebSocket applications involves several strategies. Message compression can significantly reduce bandwidth usage, especially for text-based messages. The WebSocket protocol includes an extension mechanism for per-message deflate compression, though this should be used judiciously as it increases CPU usage. Connection pooling and load balancing become important considerations when scaling WebSocket applications across multiple servers.

Browser support for WebSockets is now nearly universal, but applications should still implement fallback mechanisms for environments where WebSockets aren't available. Common fallback technologies include long polling and Server-Sent Events (SSE). However, these alternatives don't provide the same bidirectional capabilities as WebSockets and should be considered temporary solutions.

The WebSocket protocol also includes a subprotocol mechanism that allows applications to specify the format of messages that will be exchanged. This is particularly useful when building APIs that multiple clients might consume, as it allows clients to negotiate the message format during the connection handshake.

Understanding how WebSockets handle backpressure is crucial for building robust applications. Unlike HTTP, where each request-response cycle is independent, WebSocket connections must manage the flow of messages to prevent overwhelming either end of the connection. This often involves implementing queuing mechanisms and flow control strategies.

When developing WebSocket applications, tools like Chrome DevTools' Network panel and WebSocket-specific testing tools become invaluable. These tools allow developers to inspect WebSocket connections, monitor message traffic, and debug connection issues. Understanding how to use these tools effectively can significantly improve the development experience.

As we move forward into building real-time applications with Phoenix, this fundamental understanding of WebSocket technology will prove invaluable. Phoenix Channels, which we'll explore in the next chapter, builds upon these WebSocket fundamentals to provide a high-level abstraction for real-time communication, but understanding the underlying protocol helps in building more efficient and robust applications.

# 4. Introduction to Phoenix Channels

Phoenix Channels represent a powerful abstraction layer built on top of WebSocket connections, providing a robust and developer-friendly way to handle real-time communication in Phoenix applications. While WebSockets provide the foundational protocol for bidirectional communication, Channels offer a structured approach to organizing real-time features and managing client-server interactions.

At its core, a Phoenix Channel represents a topic-based communication pathway. Clients can join multiple channels, each dedicated to a specific concern or feature within your application. This separation of concerns makes it easier to organize code and manage different types of real-time interactions. For example, a chat application might have separate channels for different chat rooms, while a dashboard application might have distinct channels for different data streams.

The Channel architecture in Phoenix follows a simple yet powerful pattern. Clients join channels by subscribing to topics, which are string identifiers that define the context of the communication. When a client attempts to join a channel, the server can perform authentication and authorization checks before accepting the connection. This provides a natural point for implementing security measures and controlling access to real-time features.

Channel modules in Phoenix are structured similarly to controllers, but they handle real-time events instead of HTTP requests. A typical Channel module includes callbacks for handling various lifecycle events such as joining, leaving, and receiving messages. The join callback is particularly important as it establishes the initial connection and can set up the channel's initial state.

Messages in Phoenix Channels follow a consistent format that makes it easy to handle different types of events. Each message includes an event name and a payload, allowing you to organize your real-time functionality into discrete, meaningful interactions. The handle_in callback processes incoming messages, while handle_out manages outgoing broadcasts, providing clear separation between message types.

One of the most powerful features of Phoenix Channels is the built-in support for broadcasting messages. When a server needs to send a message to multiple clients, it can broadcast to all subscribers of a topic or send targeted messages to specific clients. This broadcasting capability is efficiently implemented using Phoenix's PubSub system, which we'll explore in more detail in later chapters.

Error handling in Channels follows Elixir's pattern matching approach, making it natural to handle different types of errors and edge cases. When a client sends a message, you can pattern match on the event name and payload to provide appropriate responses or handle errors gracefully. This makes it easy to build robust real-time features that can handle unexpected situations.

State management in Channels can be handled through process state, similar to how GenServers work. Each channel connection maintains its own state, which can be updated in response to messages or other events. This state is isolated per connection, making it easy to manage user-specific data without worrying about concurrency issues.

Channel authentication typically builds upon your application's existing authentication system. When a client attempts to join a channel, you can verify their credentials and authorize access to specific topics. This authentication can be as simple as checking a token or as complex as implementing role-based access control for different channel features.

The presence feature in Phoenix Channels provides a powerful way to track online users and handle user state across connections. Presence automatically handles the complexities of distributed state and conflict resolution, making it easy to build features that require awareness of connected users.

Testing Channel functionality is straightforward with Phoenix's testing modules. You can write tests that simulate client connections, verify message handling, and ensure your channels behave correctly under various conditions. The testing infrastructure provides tools for both unit testing individual channel functions and integration testing complete real-time features.

Performance optimization for Channels involves several considerations. Message serialization should be efficient, especially when dealing with large payloads or high message frequencies. Channel processes should be lightweight, and long-running operations should be offloaded to separate processes to maintain responsiveness.

Connection monitoring and maintenance are essential aspects of Channel management. Phoenix provides mechanisms for detecting disconnections and handling reconnection attempts. You can implement custom logic to clean up resources when clients disconnect and restore state when they reconnect, ensuring a smooth user experience even in unreliable network conditions.

Channel security extends beyond basic authentication. You should carefully consider message validation, rate limiting, and payload size restrictions to protect your application from abuse. Phoenix provides hooks for implementing these security measures at various points in the Channel lifecycle.

As your application grows, you might need to implement more sophisticated Channel architectures. This could include dynamic topic generation, channel process pooling, or custom PubSub adapters for specific scaling requirements. Phoenix's Channel system is flexible enough to accommodate these advanced use cases while maintaining its simple, elegant API.

Understanding the interaction between Channels and other Phoenix components is crucial for building effective real-time features. Channels can interact with your application's business logic, database access, and external services, but care should be taken to manage these interactions efficiently to maintain the responsiveness of your real-time features.

The development workflow for Channel-based features typically involves iterative testing using browser developer tools and Phoenix's built-in debugging capabilities. The Phoenix logger provides detailed information about channel events, making it easier to understand and debug real-time interactions during development.

As we move forward in this book, we'll build upon these Channel fundamentals to create increasingly sophisticated real-time features. The next chapter will introduce Phoenix LiveView, which provides an alternative approach to real-time functionality that can complement or replace traditional Channel-based implementations in many cases.

# 5. Phoenix LiveView Basics

Phoenix LiveView represents a revolutionary approach to building real-time web applications by enabling developers to create rich, interactive experiences without writing JavaScript. At its core, LiveView allows you to write server-rendered HTML that can be updated in real-time through WebSocket connections, all while maintaining the simplicity and productivity that Phoenix is known for.

LiveView works by establishing a persistent connection between the client and server, allowing for stateful, real-time updates to the user interface. When a LiveView is first loaded, the server renders the initial HTML and sends it to the client. After this initial render, all subsequent updates are handled through small, efficient diffs that are sent over the WebSocket connection, minimizing the amount of data transferred and providing a smooth user experience.

To create a LiveView module, you start by defining a module that uses Phoenix.LiveView and implements the required callbacks. The mount callback is particularly important as it's called when the LiveView is first initialized. This is where you set up the initial state and perform any necessary data loading. The render callback defines the HTML template that will be displayed to users, and it can access the LiveView's state to dynamically generate content.

One of the most powerful aspects of LiveView is its ability to handle user events naturally. When a user interacts with the page, such as clicking a button or submitting a form, LiveView captures these events and sends them to the server. The server can then update its state and send back only the changes that need to be applied to the DOM. This approach provides a seamless user experience while keeping the complexity of state management on the server where it's easier to reason about.

The LiveView lifecycle is straightforward but powerful. When a user first visits a LiveView page, the mount callback is called, followed by render. As users interact with the page, various callbacks are triggered to handle events and update the state. The render callback is called again whenever the state changes, allowing the view to reflect the latest data automatically.

State management in LiveView is handled through the assign function, which allows you to store and update values in the socket assigns. These assigns are then available in your templates and can be updated in response to events or other triggers. The reactive nature of LiveView means that any changes to the assigns automatically trigger a re-render of the affected portions of the page.

LiveView provides several built-in events that you can handle, such as phx-click, phx-change, and phx-submit. These events are bound to DOM elements in your template and automatically trigger corresponding event handlers in your LiveView module. For example, you might handle a button click with a phx-click binding that updates a counter in the LiveView's state.

Templates in LiveView use Phoenix's existing template system with some additional features specific to live updates. You can use regular HTML along with special LiveView bindings to create interactive interfaces. The template syntax is familiar to Phoenix developers but includes additional helpers for handling real-time updates and user interactions.

One of the key benefits of LiveView is its ability to maintain state on the server while providing immediate feedback to users. This is particularly useful for features that require complex business logic or data validation. Instead of implementing this logic in JavaScript and then duplicating it on the server, you can keep it in one place and let LiveView handle the communication.

Performance optimization in LiveView involves several considerations. The framework is designed to be efficient by default, sending only the necessary DOM updates over the wire. However, you should be mindful of the size of your LiveView's state and the frequency of updates. LiveView provides tools like temporary assigns and limit features to help manage memory usage and update frequency.

LiveView also includes powerful features for handling forms and user input. The phx-change event can provide real-time validation and feedback as users type, while phx-submit handles form submissions. These features make it easy to create interactive forms without writing any JavaScript code.

Error handling in LiveView is straightforward thanks to Elixir's pattern matching and the framework's error handling mechanisms. You can catch and handle errors at various levels, from individual event handlers to process-wide error handling. LiveView also provides hooks for handling connection errors and reconnection attempts.

Component composition is another powerful feature of LiveView. You can break down complex interfaces into smaller, reusable components using LiveComponents. These components can maintain their own state and handle their own events while still participating in the larger LiveView's lifecycle.

LiveView integrates seamlessly with Phoenix's existing authentication and authorization systems. You can protect LiveView routes using the same plugs and authentication checks you use for regular routes. Additionally, you can perform fine-grained authorization checks within the LiveView itself based on the current user's permissions.

Testing LiveView applications is straightforward using Phoenix's testing modules. You can write tests that simulate user interactions and verify that the LiveView responds correctly. The testing infrastructure provides tools for both unit testing individual LiveView functions and integration testing complete features.

As we continue through this book, we'll explore more advanced LiveView features and patterns. The next chapter will dive deeper into state management techniques and best practices for organizing complex LiveView applications. We'll see how to handle more sophisticated user interactions, manage larger state structures, and optimize performance for different types of real-time updates.

LiveView represents a significant shift in how we build interactive web applications. By keeping complexity on the server and leveraging Phoenix's powerful real-time capabilities, LiveView enables developers to create rich, interactive experiences with less code and fewer moving parts. As we progress through the book, you'll see how LiveView can be used to build everything from simple interactive elements to complex, real-time applications.

# 6. State Management in LiveView

State management is a crucial aspect of building robust LiveView applications. While LiveView simplifies many aspects of real time web development, understanding how to effectively manage state is essential for creating scalable and maintainable applications.

At its core, LiveView state is maintained in the socket assigns, which is a map like data structure that holds all the data needed to render your view. When you initialize a LiveView through the mount callback, you establish this initial state. The assign function is your primary tool for updating this state, and it's important to understand its implications.

Let's explore the various approaches to state management in LiveView. The simplest form is direct state mutation through event handlers. When a user interacts with your LiveView, you can update the state in response to these events. For example, if you're building a counter application, you might increment a value in the assigns when a user clicks a button. However, as your application grows more complex, you'll need more sophisticated state management patterns.

One important pattern is the separation of concerns in state management. Rather than keeping all state in a single LiveView, you can break it down into smaller, more focused components using LiveComponents. These components can maintain their own state while still participating in the parent LiveView's lifecycle. This approach helps manage complexity and improves code organization.

Another crucial aspect of state management is understanding the relationship between state and renders. Every time you update the state through assigns, LiveView will trigger a re-render of your template. While LiveView is optimized to send only the necessary changes to the client, frequent state updates can impact performance. It's important to structure your state updates thoughtfully to avoid unnecessary renders.

Temporary assigns provide a powerful mechanism for managing memory usage in your LiveView applications. When you have data that's only needed for the initial render and can be discarded afterwards, marking it as a temporary assign can significantly reduce memory usage. This is particularly useful when dealing with large lists or other data structures that don't need to be maintained in memory between renders.

State persistence across live navigation is another important consideration. LiveView provides mechanisms for maintaining state when users navigate between different LiveView pages. The handle_params callback allows you to update state based on URL parameters, enabling bookmarkable state and proper browser history integration.

When dealing with complex state transformations, it's often beneficial to extract the logic into separate modules. These modules can encapsulate the business logic and state transformation rules, making your LiveView code cleaner and more maintainable. This separation also makes it easier to test your state management logic independently of the LiveView.

Error handling in state management requires careful consideration. When updating state, you need to handle potential errors gracefully and ensure your LiveView remains in a consistent state. Pattern matching and case statements are your friends here, allowing you to handle different scenarios explicitly and update the state accordingly.

Real time updates from external sources present another challenge in state management. Whether you're receiving updates through PubSub or other mechanisms, you need to carefully consider how these updates integrate with your existing state. The handle_info callback is where you'll handle these external messages and update your state accordingly.

One common pattern for managing complex state is to use reducers, similar to how state is managed in frontend frameworks like Redux. You can define a set of actions that represent all possible state transitions and implement a reducer function that handles these actions. This provides a predictable way to manage state transformations and makes it easier to reason about state changes.

State initialization is another critical aspect to consider. The mount callback is where you'll typically set up your initial state, but you need to consider what happens if the initial data fetch fails or takes longer than expected. Loading states and error states should be part of your state management strategy from the beginning.

When working with forms in LiveView, form state requires special attention. The phx-change event allows you to update state as users type, enabling real time validation and feedback. However, you need to carefully consider how to manage this temporary form state versus your application's permanent state.

Caching strategies play an important role in state management. While LiveView maintains state in memory, you might need to cache certain data to improve performance or reduce database load. Consider using ETS tables or other caching mechanisms for data that's expensive to compute or fetch.

State synchronization across multiple browser tabs presents unique challenges. If users have your application open in multiple tabs, you might need to synchronize state changes across these instances. PubSub can help here, allowing you to broadcast state changes to all connected LiveView processes.

Performance optimization in state management often involves finding the right balance between responsiveness and resource usage. Techniques like debouncing state updates, batching changes, and using temporary assigns can help maintain good performance as your application scales.

Testing state management requires a comprehensive approach. Unit tests can verify your state transformation logic, while integration tests ensure that state changes correctly reflect in the rendered HTML. LiveView's testing modules provide tools for simulating user interactions and verifying state changes.

As your application grows, you might need to implement more sophisticated state management patterns. Consider using GenServers to manage shared state across multiple LiveViews, or implement CQRS patterns for complex state transformations. The key is to choose patterns that match your application's needs while maintaining code clarity and performance.

State management in LiveView is a rich topic with many considerations and best practices. By understanding these patterns and applying them appropriately, you can build maintainable, performant applications that provide excellent user experiences. In the next chapter, we'll explore how to handle forms in real time, building on these state management concepts to create interactive form experiences.

# 7. Real-Time Form Handling

Real time form handling in Phoenix LiveView revolutionizes the way we think about web forms. Unlike traditional forms that only communicate with the server upon submission, LiveView enables continuous, real time interaction that provides immediate feedback and validation to users while they type.

Let's start with the basics of form handling in LiveView. The foundation of any LiveView form is the form_for helper, which creates an HTML form that's wired up to communicate with your LiveView process. When combined with the phx-change and phx-submit bindings, you can create forms that update in real time while maintaining a clean separation between your markup and business logic.

A simple example illustrates this concept. Consider a registration form that validates a username's availability as the user types:

```elixir
def render(assigns) do
~L"""
<%= form_for @changeset, "#", [phx_change: "validate", phx_submit: "save"], fn f -> %>
<%= text_input f, :username %>
<%= error_tag f, :username %>
<%= submit "Register" %>
<% end %>
"""
end
```

The phx-change binding triggers the "validate" event as users type, allowing you to perform real time validation. This event is handled by your handle_event callback, where you can update the form's state and provide immediate feedback:

```elixir
def handle_event("validate", %{"user" => params}, socket) do
changeset =
%User{}
|> User.changeset(params)
|> Map.put(:action, :validate)
{:noreply, assign(socket, changeset: changeset)}
end
```

Form state management in LiveView typically revolves around changesets, which provide a structured way to handle form data, validation, and errors. Changesets are particularly powerful because they integrate seamlessly with Ecto and provide a consistent interface for form handling across your application.

Real time validation is one of the most powerful features of LiveView forms. Instead of waiting for a form submission to validate input, you can provide immediate feedback as users type. This might include checking for username availability, password strength, or any other custom validation rules your application requires.

When implementing real time validation, it's important to consider performance implications. You might want to debounce certain validations to avoid overwhelming your server with requests. For example, when checking username availability, you might want to wait until the user stops typing before making the database query:

```elixir
def handle_event("validate", %{"user" => params}, socket) do
if connected?(socket) do
Process.send_after(self(), {:check_username, params["username"]}, 300)
end
{:noreply, socket}
end
```

```

Form submission handling requires careful consideration of error cases and user feedback. When a form is submitted, you typically want to perform final validation, save the data, and provide appropriate feedback to the user. LiveView makes this straightforward while maintaining a great user experience:

```elixir
def handle_event("save", %{"user" => params}, socket) do
case Accounts.create_user(params) do
{:ok, user} ->
{:noreply,
socket
|> put_flash(:info, "User created successfully")
|> redirect(to: Routes.user_path(socket, :show, user))}
{:error, %Ecto.Changeset{} = changeset} ->
{:noreply, assign(socket, changeset: changeset)}
end
end
```

File uploads present unique challenges in real time applications. LiveView provides built-in support for handling file uploads through LiveView.upload_config and related functions. This enables features like progress bars, drag and drop support, and client-side file validation:

```elixir
def mount(_params, _session, socket) do
{:ok,
socket
|> assign(:uploaded_files, [])
|> allow_upload(:avatar, accept: ~w(.jpg .jpeg .png), max_entries: 1)}
end

Multi-step forms require careful state management. LiveView's ability to maintain state between renders makes it ideal for implementing wizard-like interfaces. You can track the current step in your socket assigns and render different form sections accordingly:

```elixir
def render(assigns) do
~L"""
<%= form_for @changeset, "#", [phx_change: "validate", phx_submit: "save"], fn f -> %>
<%= case @current_step do
1 -> render_step_one(f)
2 -> render_step_two(f)
3 -> render_step_three(f)
end %>
<% end %>
"""
end
```

Form accessibility is crucial and shouldn't be overlooked. LiveView's real time updates should enhance, not hinder, accessibility. This includes maintaining proper ARIA attributes, ensuring keyboard navigation works correctly, and providing clear error messages:

```elixir
def error_tag(form, field) do
if error = form.errors[field] do
content_tag(:span, translate_error(error),
class: "invalid-feedback",
phx_feedback_for: input_name(form, field),
role: "alert"
```

```
)
end
end
```

Performance optimization for forms often involves careful consideration of when to trigger updates. Not every keystroke needs to trigger a server roundtrip. Use the phx-debounce binding for inputs that don't require immediate validation:

```elixir
<%= text_input f, :email, phx_debounce: "blur" %>
```

Error handling in forms should be comprehensive and user-friendly. This includes handling network errors, validation errors, and system errors gracefully. LiveView's error boundaries can help contain errors and prevent them from crashing your entire application.

Testing form interactions is crucial for maintaining reliability. LiveView provides testing utilities that make it easy to simulate form interactions and verify behavior:

```elixir
test "validates username", %{conn: conn} do
{:ok, view, _html} = live(conn, "/register")
assert view
|> element("form")
|> render_change(%{user: %{username: ""}}) =~ "can't be blank"
end
```

Dynamic form fields present another interesting challenge. LiveView makes it easy to add and remove form fields dynamically while maintaining proper state and validation:

```elixir
def handle_event("add_field", _params, socket) do
```

```
fields = socket.assigns.fields ++ [%{id: System.unique_integer()}]
{:noreply, assign(socket, fields: fields)}
end
```

By understanding these patterns and practices for real time form handling in LiveView, you can create highly interactive, user-friendly forms that provide immediate feedback while maintaining clean, maintainable code. In the next chapter, we'll explore how to build interactive components that can be composed together to create complex user interfaces.

# 8. Building Interactive Components

Building interactive components in Phoenix LiveView opens up new possibilities for creating dynamic, reusable user interface elements. Components in LiveView are more than just templates; they are stateful, isolated pieces of functionality that can be composed together to build complex interfaces while maintaining clean, maintainable code.

LiveView components come in two main varieties: stateless and stateful. Stateless components are simpler and function similarly to traditional function components, while stateful components maintain their own state and lifecycle. Let's explore both types and their use cases.

A stateless component is perfect for simple UI elements that don't need to maintain their own state. These are defined using the defp render_component pattern and can be called directly from your templates:

```elixir
defmodule MyAppWeb.CardComponent do
use Phoenix.Component
def card(assigns) do
~H"""
<div class="card">
<div class="card-header">
<%= @title %>
</div>
<div class="card-body">
<%= render_slot(@inner_block) %>
</div>
</div>
"""
end
```

```
end
```

Stateful components, on the other hand, are more powerful and can maintain their own state, handle events, and manage their own lifecycle. These are defined using Phoenix.LiveComponent and can be rendered using live_component:

```elixir
defmodule MyAppWeb.CounterComponent do
use Phoenix.LiveComponent
def mount(socket) do
{:ok, assign(socket, count: 0)}
end
def render(assigns) do
~H"""
<div>
Count: <%= @count %>
<button phx-click="increment" phx-target="<%= @myself %>">+</button>
</div>
"""
end
def handle_event("increment", _, socket) do
{:noreply, update(socket, :count, &(&1 + 1))}
end
end
```

Component communication is a crucial aspect of building interactive interfaces. LiveView provides several mechanisms for components to communicate with each other and their parent LiveView. The send_update function allows you to trigger updates in other components:

```elixir
```

```
def handle_event("update_counter", _, socket) do
send_update CounterComponent, id: "counter1", count: 10
{:noreply, socket}
end
```

Slots provide a powerful way to compose components and pass content between them. They work similarly to traditional HTML slots but with the full power of LiveView:

```elixir
def modal(assigns) do
~H"""
<div class="modal">
<div class="modal-header">
<%= render_slot(@header) %>
</div>
<div class="modal-body">
<%= render_slot(@inner_block) %>
</div>
<div class="modal-footer">
<%= render_slot(@footer) %>
</div>
</div>
"""
end
```

Component lifecycle management is important for proper resource cleanup and initialization. LiveView components can implement lifecycle callbacks like mount, update, and preload:

```elixir
defmodule MyAppWeb.ChartComponent do
use Phoenix.LiveComponent
def mount(socket) do
```

```
{:ok, assign(socket, chart_data: [], loading: true)}
end
def update(assigns, socket) do
if connected?(socket) and socket.assigns.loading do
{:ok, fetch_chart_data(socket)}
else
{:ok, assign(socket, assigns)}
end
end
def preload(list_of_assigns) do
# Preload data for multiple instances of the component
Enum.map(list_of_assigns, &Map.put(&1, :preloaded_data, fetch_preload_data(&1)))
end
end
```

Performance optimization for components often involves careful consideration of when components should update. The function_component macro can help create highly optimized stateless components:

```elixir
def function_component(:user_card, assigns) do
~H"""
<div class="user-card">
<img src={@user.avatar_url} />
<h3><%= @user.name %></h3>
<p><%= @user.bio %></p>
</div>
"""
end
```

Component testing is crucial for maintaining reliability. LiveView provides testing utilities specifically designed for components:

```elixir
test "counter increments when clicked", %{conn: conn} do
{:ok, view, _html} = live(conn, "/")
assert view
|> element("#counter-1 button")
|> render_click() =~ "Count: 1"
end
```

Error handling in components should be robust and user-friendly. Components can implement their own error boundaries to contain and handle errors gracefully:

```elixir
def render(assigns) do
~H"""
<div phx-hook="ErrorBoundary" id={@id}>
<%= if @error do %>
<div class="error-message">
Something went wrong: <%= @error %>
</div>
<% else %>
<%= render_content(assigns) %>
<% end %>
</div>
"""
end
```

Real time updates in components often require careful state management. The temporary_assigns option can help manage memory usage for components that handle large lists or frequently changing data:

```elixir
def mount(socket) do
{:ok, socket, temporary_assigns: [messages: []]}
end
```

Component composition allows you to build complex interfaces from smaller, reusable pieces. This might include nested components, shared behaviors, and common patterns:

```elixir
def render(assigns) do
~H"""
<.card>
<:header>
<.user_avatar user={@user} />
<.user_name user={@user} />
</:header>
<.user_stats user={@user} />
<:footer>
<.action_buttons user={@user} />
</:footer>
</.card>
"""
end
```

By mastering these component patterns and practices, you can create sophisticated, interactive interfaces while maintaining code organization and reusability. Components form the building blocks of modern LiveView applications, enabling rapid development of complex features while keeping code maintainable and performant.

# 9. LiveView Event Handling

Chapter 9 focuses on LiveView event handling, a crucial aspect of building interactive web applications with Phoenix LiveView. Events form the backbone of user interactions, allowing applications to respond to user actions in real time without full page reloads.

LiveView provides several mechanisms for handling events, with the most common being phx-click, phx-change, and phx-submit. These event bindings can be attached to any HTML element and trigger corresponding handle_event callbacks in your LiveView module.

The basic structure of event handling starts with the event binding in your template:

```elixir
<button phx-click="increment">Increment</button>
<form phx-change="validate" phx-submit="save">
<input type="text" name="username" value={@username} />
<button type="submit">Save</button>
</form>
```

When these events are triggered, they are handled by corresponding callbacks in your LiveView:

```elixir
def handle_event("increment", _params, socket) do
{:noreply, update(socket, :count, &(&1 + 1))}
end
def handle_event("validate", %{"username" => username}, socket) do
{:noreply, assign(socket, username: username)}
end
def handle_event("save", %{"username" => username}, socket) do
```

```
{:noreply, socket |> put_flash(:info, "Saved!") |> assign(:username, username)}
end
```

Event metadata provides additional context about the event, including the target element, any modifier keys pressed, and other relevant information. This metadata can be accessed through the second parameter of handle_event:

```elixir
def handle_event("keydown", %{"key" => key, "metaKey" => meta_key}, socket) do
if meta_key and key == "s" do
# Handle save shortcut
{:noreply, save_document(socket)}
else
{:noreply, socket}
end
end
```

Debouncing and throttling are important considerations when handling events that might fire rapidly, such as text input or mouse movement. LiveView provides built in support for debouncing through the phx-debounce binding:

```elixir
<input type="text"
name="search"
phx-change="search"
phx-debounce="300"
value={@search_term} />
```

Event targeting allows you to specify which LiveView or component should handle an event. This is particularly useful when working with nested components:

```elixir
<div phx-target={@myself} phx-click="handle_click">
Click me to update only this component
</div>
```

Window and document level events can be handled using phx-window-* and phx-document-* bindings. These are useful for implementing keyboard shortcuts or handling scroll events:

```elixir
<div phx-window-keydown="handle_keydown"
phx-window-scroll="handle_scroll">
<!—Content—>
</div>
```

Custom events can be pushed from JavaScript using the push_event function provided by the LiveView JavaScript library:

```javascript
let liveSocket = new LiveSocket("/live", Socket, {
hooks: {
CustomEvent: {
mounted() {
this.pushEvent("custom_event", {data: "value"})
}
}
}
})
```

Error handling in events should be robust and provide good user feedback. LiveView makes it easy to handle errors and display appropriate messages:

```elixir
def handle_event("save", params, socket) do
case save_data(params) do
{:ok, _data} ->
{:noreply, put_flash(socket, :info, "Saved successfully!")}
{:error, changeset} ->
{:noreply,
socket
|> put_flash(:error, "Failed to save")
|> assign(:changeset, changeset)}
end
end
```

Event propagation can be controlled using phx-stop-propagation and phx-prevent-default. These are particularly useful when working with nested elements that might trigger multiple events:

```elixir
<div phx-click="outer">
<button phx-click="inner" phx-stop-propagation>
Click me
</button>
</div>
```

Rate limiting can be implemented at the event level to prevent abuse or excessive server load:

```elixir
def handle_event("expensive_operation", _params, socket) do
if rate_limit_exceeded?(socket) do
```

```
{:noreply, put_flash(socket, :error, "Please wait before trying again")}
else
{:noreply, perform_expensive_operation(socket)}
end
end
```

Event handling can also interact with browser navigation through pushState and replaceState:

```elixir
def handle_event("navigate", %{"path" => path}, socket) do
{:noreply, push_patch(socket, to: path)}
end
```

Complex interactions often require coordinating multiple events and state updates. It's important to maintain clean, organized code when handling related events:

```elixir
defmodule MyAppWeb.FormLive do
use MyAppWeb, :live_view
def mount(_params, _session, socket) do
{:ok, assign(socket, form_data: %{}, validation_errors: %{})}
end
def handle_event("validate", %{"form" => form_data}, socket) do
validation_errors = validate_form(form_data)
{:noreply, assign(socket, form_data: form_data, validation_errors: validation_errors)}
end
def handle_event("save", %{"form" => form_data}, socket) do
case save_form_data(form_data) do
{:ok, _} -> {:noreply, redirect(socket, to: "/")}
```

```
{:error, errors} ->
{:noreply,
socket
|> assign(validation_errors: errors)
|> put_flash(:error, "Please correct the errors")}
end
end
defp validate_form(data) do
# Validation logic
end
defp save_form_data(data) do
# Save logic
end
end
```

Understanding and effectively implementing event handling in LiveView is crucial for building responsive, interactive applications. By leveraging LiveView's event handling capabilities, you can create rich user experiences while maintaining clean, maintainable code that scales well as your application grows.

# 10. Client-Side Interactivity with Hooks

Client-side interactivity in Phoenix LiveView can be significantly enhanced through the use of hooks, which provide a bridge between LiveView's server-side logic and client-side JavaScript functionality. Hooks enable developers to integrate custom JavaScript behavior while maintaining the benefits of LiveView's server-driven architecture.

Hooks are defined in JavaScript and can be attached to DOM elements using the phx-hook attribute. They provide several lifecycle callbacks that allow you to execute code at specific points during an element's lifecycle. Let's explore how to implement and utilize hooks effectively.

To get started with hooks, you first need to define them when initializing your LiveSocket:

```javascript
let Hooks = {}
Hooks.MyHook = {
mounted() {
// Called when the element is added to the DOM
console.log("Element mounted", this.el)
},
destroyed() {
// Called when the element is removed from the DOM
console.log("Element destroyed")
},
updated() {
// Called when the element's attributes are updated
console.log("Element updated")
}
}
let liveSocket = new LiveSocket("/live", Socket, {
```

```
hooks: Hooks,
params: {_csrf_token: csrfToken}
})
```

Once defined, hooks can be attached to elements in your LiveView templates using the phx-hook attribute:

```elixir
<div id="my-element" phx-hook="MyHook">
Content that needs custom JavaScript behavior
</div>
```

One common use case for hooks is integrating third-party JavaScript libraries. For example, let's implement a hook that initializes a chart using Chart.js:

```javascript
Hooks.Chart = {
mounted() {
const ctx = this.el.getContext('2d')
this.chart = new Chart(ctx, {
type: 'line',
data: JSON.parse(this.el.dataset.chartData),
options: {
responsive: true
}
})
this.handleEvent("update_chart_data", ({data}) => {
this.chart.data = data
this.chart.update()
})
},
destroyed() {
this.chart.destroy()
```

```
}
}
```

Hooks can also be used to handle DOM events that LiveView doesn't natively support or require complex JavaScript interaction. For instance, implementing drag and drop functionality:

```javascript
Hooks.DragDrop = {
mounted() {
this.el.addEventListener('dragstart', e => {
e.dataTransfer.setData('text/plain', e.target.id)
})
this.el.addEventListener('dragover', e => {
e.preventDefault()
})
this.el.addEventListener('drop', e => {
e.preventDefault()
const id = e.dataTransfer.getData('text/plain')
this.pushEvent("item_dropped", {
dragged_id: id,
dropped_id: e.target.id
})
})
}
}
```

Hooks provide several methods for communicating between JavaScript and LiveView. The pushEvent method sends events to the server, while handleEvent listens for events from the server:

```javascript
Hooks.Messenger = {
mounted() {
```

```
// Send events to the server
this.pushEvent("client_ready", {browser: navigator.userAgent})
// Receive events from the server
this.handleEvent("server_message", ({message}) => {
console.log("Received message:", message)
})
}
}
```

Sometimes you need to coordinate between multiple hooks on a page. This can be accomplished by implementing a pub/sub system using hook callbacks:

```javascript
const PubSub = {
subscribers: {},
subscribe(event, callback) {
if (!this.subscribers[event]) {
this.subscribers[event] = []
}
this.subscribers[event].push(callback)
},
publish(event, data) {
if (this.subscribers[event]) {
this.subscribers[event].forEach(callback => callback(data))
}
}
}
Hooks.Publisher = {
mounted() {
this.el.addEventListener('click', () => {
PubSub.publish('buttonClicked', {
timestamp: new Date()
```

```
})
})
}
}
Hooks.Subscriber = {
mounted() {
PubSub.subscribe('buttonClicked', (data) => {
console.log('Button was clicked at:', data.timestamp)
})
}
}
```

Hooks can also be used to manage complex form interactions, such as handling file uploads with preview functionality:

```javascript
Hooks.FileUpload = {
mounted() {
this.el.addEventListener('change', (e) => {
const file = e.target.files[0]
const reader = new FileReader()
reader.onload = (e) => {
const preview = document.getElementById('preview')
preview.src = e.target.result
this.pushEvent("file_selected", {
filename: file.name,
type: file.type,
size: file.size
})
}
reader.readAsDataURL(file)
})
}
```

```
}
```

When working with hooks that involve expensive operations or event listeners, it's important to properly clean up resources in the destroyed callback:

```javascript
Hooks.ResourceIntensive = {
mounted() {
this.interval = setInterval(() => {
// Perform periodic operations
}, 1000)
this.observer = new IntersectionObserver(entries => {
// Handle intersection events
})
this.observer.observe(this.el)
},
destroyed() {
clearInterval(this.interval)
this.observer.disconnect()
}
}
```

Hooks can also be used to implement infinite scrolling or lazy loading functionality:

```javascript
Hooks.InfiniteScroll = {
mounted() {
const observer = new IntersectionObserver(entries => {
entries.forEach(entry => {
if (entry.isIntersecting) {
this.pushEvent("load_more", {})
}
```

```
})
})
observer.observe(this.el)
}
}
```

Error handling in hooks is important to ensure robust client-side behavior:

```javascript
Hooks.ErrorAware = {
mounted() {
try {
// Potentially dangerous operation
this.initializeComponent()
} catch (error) {
console.error("Failed to initialize component:", error)
this.pushEvent("initialization_failed", {
error: error.message
})
}
}
}
```

By effectively using hooks, you can create rich, interactive user experiences while maintaining the benefits of LiveView's server-driven architecture. The key is to find the right balance between server-side and client-side functionality, using hooks when necessary to bridge the gap between the two worlds.

# 11. Phoenix PubSub Fundamentals

Phoenix PubSub serves as the backbone of real-time communication in Phoenix applications, providing a distributed publish-subscribe system that enables seamless message broadcasting across channels, LiveViews, and even between different nodes in a distributed system. Understanding PubSub fundamentals is crucial for building scalable real-time applications.

At its core, Phoenix PubSub implements the publish-subscribe pattern, where publishers broadcast messages to topics, and subscribers receive messages from topics they're interested in. This decoupling of publishers and subscribers creates a flexible and scalable architecture for real-time applications.

To start using PubSub in your Phoenix application, you'll first need to ensure it's properly configured. In a typical Phoenix application, PubSub is automatically configured in your application supervision tree. The configuration usually looks something like this in your application.ex file:

```elixir
def start(_type, _args) do
children = [
{Phoenix.PubSub, name: MyApp.PubSub},
# other children...
]
opts = [strategy: :one_for_one, name: MyApp.Supervisor]
Supervisor.start_link(children, opts)
end
```

The basic operations in PubSub are subscribe and broadcast. Subscribing to a topic is straightforward and can be done from any process in your application. When subscribing, you specify a topic name, which is typically a string that represents what you're interested in receiving messages about:

```elixir
Phoenix.PubSub.subscribe(MyApp.PubSub,
"user:123:notifications")
```

Broadcasting messages is equally simple. You can broadcast a message to all subscribers of a topic:

```elixir
Phoenix.PubSub.broadcast(MyApp.PubSub,
"user:123:notifications", {:new_notification, %{text: "Hello!"}})
```

One of the powerful features of Phoenix PubSub is its support for pattern matching in message handling. When you receive a message, you can pattern match on its structure to handle different types of messages differently:

```elixir
def handle_info({:new_notification, payload}, socket) do
{:noreply, assign(socket, :notifications, [payload |
socket.assigns.notifications])}
end
def handle_info({:notification_deleted, notification_id},
socket) do
notifications = Enum.reject(socket.assigns.notifications,
&(&1.id == notification_id))
{:noreply, assign(socket, :notifications, notifications)}
end
```

PubSub also supports local broadcasting, which only delivers messages to subscribers on the same node. This can be useful when you want to optimize performance for certain types of messages:

```elixir
```

```
Phoenix.PubSub.local_broadcast(MyApp.PubSub,
"local_topic", {:local_event, data})
```

When building real-time features, it's common to need to track which processes are subscribed to which topics. PubSub provides functionality to help with this through its tracker feature. The tracker helps maintain a list of processes and their associated metadata across a distributed system:

```elixir
defmodule MyApp.Presence do
use Phoenix.Presence,
otp_app: :my_app,
pubsub_server: MyApp.PubSub
end
```

Topics in PubSub can be organized hierarchically, allowing for flexible message routing patterns. A common pattern is to use colon-separated strings to represent topic hierarchies:

```elixir
# Subscribe to all messages for a specific user
Phoenix.PubSub.subscribe(MyApp.PubSub, "user:123:*")
# Subscribe to all chat messages in a specific room
Phoenix.PubSub.subscribe(MyApp.PubSub,
"chat:room:456:messages")
```

When working with LiveView, PubSub integration is particularly powerful. You can subscribe to topics in the mount callback and update the UI automatically when messages arrive:

```elixir
def mount(_params, _session, socket) do
if connected?(socket) do
Phoenix.PubSub.subscribe(MyApp.PubSub, "updates")
```

```
end
{:ok, assign(socket, :messages, [])}
end
```

PubSub can also be used to implement real-time search functionality. As users type, you can broadcast their search terms and update results in real-time:

```elixir
def handle_event("search", %{"query" => query}, socket) do
Phoenix.PubSub.broadcast(MyApp.PubSub, "search:results", {:search, query})
{:noreply, socket}
end
```

Error handling is an important consideration when working with PubSub. Since message delivery is asynchronous, you should handle potential failures gracefully:

```elixir
def broadcast_safely(topic, message) do
try do
Phoenix.PubSub.broadcast(MyApp.PubSub, topic, message)
rescue
error ->
Logger.error("Failed to broadcast message: #{inspect(error)}")
{:error, :broadcast_failed}
end
end
```

When building larger applications, you might want to implement a PubSub facade module to encapsulate your publication and subscription logic:

```elixir
```

```
defmodule MyApp.Realtime do
def subscribe_to_user_events(user_id) do
Phoenix.PubSub.subscribe(MyApp.PubSub, "user:#{user_id}:events")
end
def broadcast_user_event(user_id, event) do
Phoenix.PubSub.broadcast(MyApp.PubSub, "user:#{user_id}:events", {:user_event, event})
end
def unsubscribe_from_user_events(user_id) do
Phoenix.PubSub.unsubscribe(MyApp.PubSub, "user:#{user_id}:events")
end
end
```

PubSub's distributed nature becomes particularly valuable when scaling your application across multiple nodes. Messages are automatically distributed to subscribers across all connected nodes:

```elixir
defmodule MyApp.Cluster do
def broadcast_to_cluster(message) do
Phoenix.PubSub.broadcast(MyApp.PubSub, "cluster:events", {:cluster_event, message})
end
end
```

Understanding Phoenix PubSub fundamentals is essential for building scalable real-time applications. It provides the communication infrastructure needed for features like chat systems, real-time dashboards, and collaborative tools. By effectively utilizing PubSub's features and patterns, you can create responsive and resilient applications that can scale across multiple nodes while maintaining consistent real-time behavior.

# 12. Building a Chat Application

Building real-time chat applications is one of the most compelling use cases for Phoenix and its WebSocket capabilities. In this chapter, we'll create a production-ready chat application that showcases Phoenix's strengths in handling real-time communication at scale. By the end, you'll understand how to architect and implement a robust chat system that can support thousands of concurrent users while maintaining crisp performance.

Real-time chat presents unique challenges that make it an excellent learning opportunity. We need to handle concurrent connections, maintain consistent state across distributed nodes, persist messages reliably, and provide a responsive user experience. Phoenix gives us powerful tools to address these challenges: Channels for WebSocket communication, PubSub for message broadcasting, Presence for user tracking, and LiveView for dynamic UI updates.

Our chat application will follow a layered architecture that separates concerns and promotes maintainability. At the core, we'll use Phoenix Channels to handle WebSocket connections and message distribution. Above that, we'll implement a PubSub system to broadcast messages across server nodes. For persistence, we'll store messages in PostgreSQL, using Ecto for database interactions. The application will support multiple chat rooms, each maintaining its own message history and participant list. Users can join multiple rooms, and the system will track their presence in each one. We'll implement typing indicators and read receipts to enhance the user experience.

We'll start by creating a new Phoenix project with LiveView support. After running mix phx.new chat_app—live and setting up our database with mix ecto.create, we'll begin implementing our core functionality. The foundation of our chat system lies in its database schema design. We need to consider both real-time performance and message persistence.

For our database structure, we'll create two primary schemas: Room and Message. The Room schema will store information about each chat room, including its name, topic, and references to its messages. The Message schema will store the actual chat messages, including the sender, content, timestamp, and any additional metadata like read receipts.

In the Room schema, we include fields for the room's name and topic, along with a has_many relationship to messages. We implement a changeset function to validate room creation, ensuring each room has a unique name. This prevents confusion and potential conflicts in our system.

The Message schema is more complex, containing fields for the message content, sender information, timestamps, and read status. We'll include a belongs_to relationship back to the room, creating a two-way association that allows efficient querying of messages by room.

To handle presence tracking, we'll leverage Phoenix's built-in Presence module. This will maintain a real-time list of users in each room, handling node failures and network partitions gracefully. The Presence system will track not just who's online, but also metadata like typing status and last activity timestamp.

Each chat room will be backed by a dedicated GenServer process that manages room state and handles message broadcasting. This process will coordinate with Phoenix PubSub to ensure messages are distributed to all connected clients, even across multiple server nodes. The GenServer will also maintain a message buffer for performance optimization, reducing database load for recent messages.

For the communication layer, we'll implement a ChatChannel module that handles WebSocket connections. This channel will manage client subscriptions to rooms, broadcast messages, and coordinate presence updates. We'll implement message throttling and rate limiting to prevent abuse and ensure system stability under load.

The front end will use LiveView to create a responsive, real-time user interface. LiveView's server-rendered approach means we can build rich interactive features without complex client-side JavaScript. We'll implement features like typing indicators and message status updates using LiveView's real-time update capabilities.

# 13. Handling User Presence

User presence is a critical feature in real-time applications. Whether you're building a chat system, a collaborative document editor, or a multiplayer game, users need to know who else is currently active. Phoenix Presence provides powerful primitives for tracking user state across distributed systems, handling node failures gracefully, and maintaining consistency without a central data store.

• • • •

IN TRADITIONAL APPLICATIONS, tracking user presence often involves storing state in a database or cache. This approach breaks down in distributed systems where multiple servers need consistent, real-time presence information. Phoenix Presence solves this through a conflict-free replicated data type (CRDT) implementation, enabling automatic state synchronization across nodes without requiring consensus protocols.

• • • •

THE MAGIC OF PHOENIX Presence lies in its automatic conflict resolution. When network partitions occur or nodes fail, Presence automatically reconciles state differences when connectivity is restored. This self-healing behavior means developers don't need to write complex conflict resolution logic - Presence handles edge cases automatically.

• • • •

LET'S EXTEND OUR CHAT application to track user presence. We'll show who's online in each room, display typing indicators, and implement "last seen" timestamps. We'll start by adding Presence to our application. The first step is defining a Presence module that will track user state. This module builds on Phoenix.Presence and configures our PubSub system for presence tracking.

• • • •

OUR PRESENCE MODULE serves as the central coordination point for presence information. It tracks which users are online in which rooms, maintains metadata about each user's state, and broadcasts changes to all connected clients. The module handles joining and leaving events, updates to user metadata (like typing status), and periodic heartbeat checks to ensure presence information stays current.

• • • •

EACH USER'S PRESENCE is tracked with a rich metadata structure. Beyond simple online/offline status, we store information like their current activity, device type, and last active timestamp. This metadata enables features like showing when someone is typing or indicating if they're on mobile versus desktop. The metadata is automatically distributed to all nodes in the cluster, ensuring consistent presence information everywhere.

• • • •

FOR TYPING INDICATORS, we implement a debounced presence update system. When a user starts typing, we update their presence metadata with a typing status. After a short delay without further typing, we clear this status. This approach provides real-time feedback while avoiding excessive presence updates that could impact system performance.

• • • •

TO HANDLE USER SESSIONS across multiple devices, we implement presence tracking at both the user and device level. A single user can have multiple presence entries, one for each connected device. When displaying online status, we aggregate these entries to show appropriate status information - for example, showing a user as "online on mobile" even if they're offline on desktop.

• • • •

PERFORMANCE CONSIDERATIONS are crucial when implementing presence features. Each presence update triggers a broadcast to all connected clients, so we need to carefully manage update frequency. We implement rate limiting for presence updates and batch updates when possible to reduce system load. For rooms with many users, we paginate the presence list and implement lazy loading to maintain responsive performance.

• • • •

FAULT TOLERANCE IS a key consideration in our presence system. When a node fails, Phoenix Presence automatically redistributes its presence tracking responsibilities to other nodes. Similarly, when a node comes back online, it automatically receives the current presence state from existing nodes. This self-healing behavior ensures our presence system remains reliable even during infrastructure issues.

• • • •

TO HANDLE TEMPORARY disconnects gracefully, we implement a presence grace period. When a user's connection drops, we don't immediately mark them as offline. Instead, we wait for a configurable period to see if they reconnect. This prevents presence information from flapping during brief network interruptions, providing a better user experience.

• • • •

THE PRESENCE SYSTEM also helps with cleanup tasks. When a user's presence entries expire, we can trigger cleanup actions like marking messages as unread or notifying other users of their departure. We implement these cleanup tasks as callbacks in our Presence module, ensuring they run consistently across all nodes.

• • • •

FOR MONITORING AND debugging, we implement presence tracking telemetry. We emit metrics for presence joins, leaves, and updates, allowing us to monitor system health and detect unusual patterns. These metrics help us understand how users interact with our application and identify potential performance bottlenecks.

• • • •

FINALLY, WE IMPLEMENT presence list caching to optimize performance for rooms with many users. Instead of calculating the full presence list on every request, we maintain a cached version that updates incrementally as presence changes occur. This significantly reduces the computational overhead of presence tracking in large rooms.

• • • •

THROUGH THESE IMPLEMENTATIONS, we create a robust presence system that scales reliably across distributed deployments. Phoenix Presence handles the complex distributed systems challenges, letting us focus on building features that enhance user experience. The result is a presence system that's both powerful and maintainable, providing real-time presence information that users can trust.

# 14. Real-Time Dashboard Architecture

Building a real-time dashboard architecture requires careful consideration of data flow, state management, and performance optimization. In this chapter, we'll explore the fundamental principles and implementation details of creating scalable dashboards using Phoenix LiveView and WebSocket connections.

Real-time dashboards present unique challenges compared to traditional web applications. They need to handle continuous data updates, maintain responsiveness under heavy load, and provide an excellent user experience while managing potentially large amounts of streaming data. The architecture we'll discuss focuses on these requirements while leveraging Elixir's concurrent processing capabilities.

At the core of our dashboard architecture is the concept of data producers and consumers. Producers might include IoT devices, system metrics, user activities, or external APIs that generate real-time data. Consumers are typically dashboard components that display this information through charts, tables, or other visualizations. The key is to establish efficient communication channels between these entities while maintaining system stability.

Let's start with the basic structure of a dashboard LiveView module:

```elixir
defmodule MyAppWeb.DashboardLive do
use MyAppWeb, :live_view
alias MyApp.Metrics
alias Phoenix.PubSub
def mount(_params, _session, socket) do
if connected?(socket) do
PubSub.subscribe(MyApp.PubSub, "dashboard_updates")
schedule_metrics_update()
```

```
end
{:ok, assign(socket, metrics: get_initial_metrics())}
end
end
```

This foundation allows us to establish WebSocket connections and begin receiving real-time updates. However, the real challenge lies in managing data flow and preventing overwhelming the client with updates. We need to implement intelligent data buffering and throttling mechanisms.

One effective pattern is to use GenServers as data aggregators. These processes can collect and process incoming data before broadcasting it to connected dashboard clients. This approach helps prevent flooding the system with excessive messages while ensuring data consistency:

```elixir
defmodule MyApp.MetricsAggregator do
use GenServer
def start_link(_opts) do
GenServer.start_link(__MODULE__, %{}, name: __MODULE__)
end
def init(state) do
schedule_broadcast()
{:ok, state}
end
def handle_info(:broadcast, state) do
Phoenix.PubSub.broadcast(MyApp.PubSub, "dashboard_updates", {:metrics_update, aggregate_metrics(state)})
schedule_broadcast()
{:noreply, %{}}
end
```

```
end
```

Another crucial aspect of dashboard architecture is handling different update frequencies for various components. Some metrics might need real-time updates every second, while others could be updated less frequently. We can implement multiple PubSub topics and control update frequencies at the component level:

```elixir
def handle_info({:metrics_update, metrics}, socket) do
metrics = apply_update_strategy(metrics, socket.assigns.update_frequency)
{:noreply, assign(socket, :metrics, metrics)}
end
defp apply_update_strategy(metrics, :realtime), do: metrics
defp apply_update_strategy(metrics, :throttled) do
Process.send_after(self(), {:delayed_update, metrics}, 5000)
socket.assigns.metrics
end
```

Memory management becomes crucial when dealing with real-time dashboards. We need to implement efficient data structures and cleanup mechanisms to prevent memory leaks. One approach is to use ETS tables for temporary data storage and implement automatic cleanup:

```elixir
def handle_info(:cleanup_old_data, socket) do
:ets.select_delete(:dashboard_metrics,
[{{:_, :"$2"}, [{:<, :"$2", :os.system_time(:second) - 3600}], [true]}])
schedule_cleanup()
{:noreply, socket}
end
```

```

To ensure dashboard scalability, we should implement data partitioning and lazy loading strategies. Instead of loading all dashboard data at once, we can load data incrementally based on user interaction and viewport visibility:

```elixir
def handle_event("load_more_data", %{"section" => section}, socket) do
metrics = load_section_metrics(section, socket.assigns.page_size)
{:noreply, update(socket, :metrics, &Map.merge(&1, metrics))}
end
```

Error handling and recovery mechanisms are essential for maintaining dashboard reliability. We should implement circuit breakers and fallback mechanisms for data sources:

```elixir
def fetch_metrics_with_fallback do
try do
Metrics.fetch_latest()
rescue
error ->
Logger.error("Failed to fetch metrics: #{inspect(error)}")
get_cached_metrics()
end
end
```

Another important consideration is the implementation of real-time filtering and aggregation capabilities. Users often need to analyze data in different ways, and our architecture should support this without sacrificing performance:

```elixir

```
def handle_event("apply_filter", %{"filter" => filter}, socket) do
filtered_metrics = apply_metric_filters(socket.assigns.metrics, filter)
{:noreply, assign(socket, :filtered_metrics, filtered_metrics)}
end
defp apply_metric_filters(metrics, filter) do
Enum.reduce(metrics, %{}, fn {key, value}, acc ->
if meets_filter_criteria?(value, filter) do
Map.put(acc, key, value)
else
acc
end
end)
end
```

Performance optimization is crucial for real-time dashboards. We should implement efficient data structures and caching mechanisms to minimize processing overhead:

```elixir
defmodule MyApp.DashboardCache do
use GenServer
def get_cached_metrics(key) do
case :ets.lookup(:dashboard_cache, key) do
[{^key, value, timestamp}] when timestamp > expiration_threshold() ->
value
_ ->
fetch_and_cache_metrics(key)
end
end
end
```

Finally, we need to consider the impact of connection drops and reconnection handling. The dashboard should gracefully handle disconnections and restore state when connections are reestablished:

```elixir
def handle_info({:live_view_disconnected, _reason}, socket) do
Process.send_after(self(), :attempt_reconnect, 5000)
{:noreply, assign(socket, :connection_status, :disconnected)}
end
def handle_info(:attempt_reconnect, socket) do
case reconnect_to_services() do
{:ok, fresh_data} ->
{:noreply, assign(socket, connection_status: :connected,
metrics: fresh_data)}
{:error, _reason} ->
Process.send_after(self(), :attempt_reconnect, 5000)
{:noreply, socket}
end
end
```

By implementing these architectural patterns and considerations, we can create robust and scalable real-time dashboards that provide excellent user experiences while maintaining system stability and performance. The key is to balance real-time updates with system resources and user needs, implementing appropriate buffering, caching, and error handling mechanisms throughout the application.

Remember that dashboard architecture is not one-size-fits-all, and you should adjust these patterns based on your specific requirements, data volumes, and user expectations. Regular monitoring and performance testing will help you fine-tune these implementations for optimal results.

# 15. Data Visualization with LiveView

Data visualization is a crucial aspect of real-time applications, and Phoenix LiveView provides powerful tools for creating dynamic, interactive visualizations that update in real-time. In this chapter, we'll explore various approaches to implementing data visualization using LiveView, focusing on both performance and user experience.

When implementing data visualization in LiveView, we need to consider both server-side data processing and client-side rendering capabilities. Modern JavaScript libraries like Chart.js, D3.js, or ApexCharts can be seamlessly integrated with LiveView to create compelling visualizations while maintaining the real-time aspect of our application.

Let's start by implementing a basic chart component using LiveView and Chart.js. First, we'll create a LiveView module that handles the data and rendering:

```elixir
defmodule MyAppWeb.ChartLive do
use MyAppWeb, :live_view
alias MyApp.TimeSeriesData
def mount(_params, _session, socket) do
if connected?(socket) do
Phoenix.PubSub.subscribe(MyApp.PubSub, "chart_updates")
schedule_data_update()
end
initial_data = TimeSeriesData.get_initial_dataset()
{:ok, assign(socket, dataset: initial_data, chart_options: default_chart_options())}
end
end
```

The visualization process typically involves several key aspects: data preparation, chart configuration, and update handling. For time series data, we often need to implement windowing and aggregation functions to maintain performance with large datasets:

```elixir
def prepare_time_series_data(raw_data, window_size) do
raw_data
|> Enum.chunk_every(window_size)
|> Enum.map(fn chunk ->
%{
timestamp: mean_timestamp(chunk),
value: Enum.average(chunk, & &1.value)
}
end)
end
```

One of the challenges with real-time visualization is managing update frequency without overwhelming the browser or creating a janky user experience. We can implement smart update batching:

```elixir
def handle_info({:new_datapoint, point}, socket) do
socket =
update(socket, :dataset, fn dataset ->
updated = [point | dataset]
if length(updated) > 1000 do
Enum.take(updated, 1000)
else
updated
end
end)
if should_push_update?(socket) do
```

```
{:noreply, push_event(socket, "chartUpdate", %{data: prepare_chart_data(socket.assigns.dataset)})}
else
{:noreply, socket}
end
end
```

For more complex visualizations, we might need to implement custom JavaScript hooks to handle specialized rendering requirements:

```javascript
let Hooks = {}
Hooks.Chart = {
mounted() {
this.chart = new Chart(this.el, {
type: 'line',
data: this.buildChartData({}),
options: this.buildChartOptions()
})
this.handleEvent("chartUpdate", (payload) => {
this.updateChart(payload.data)
})
},
updateChart(newData) {
this.chart.data.datasets = newData
this.chart.update('active')
}
}
```

When dealing with large datasets, we need to implement efficient data structures and update strategies. One approach is to use circular buffers for time series data:

```elixir
defmodule MyApp.CircularBuffer do
defstruct [:data, :max_size, :current_index]
def new(max_size) do
%__MODULE__{
data: :array.new(max_size),
max_size: max_size,
current_index: 0
}
end
def push(buffer, value) do
new_index = rem(buffer.current_index + 1, buffer.max_size)
new_data = :array.set(buffer.current_index, value, buffer.data)
%{buffer | data: new_data, current_index: new_index}
end
end
```

Interactive visualizations often require handling user interactions and filtering. We can implement these features while maintaining real-time updates:

```elixir
def handle_event("filter_data", %{"range" => range}, socket) do
filtered_data = apply_time_range_filter(socket.assigns.dataset, range)
{:noreply, assign(socket, :filtered_dataset, filtered_data)}
end
def handle_event("zoom", %{"level" => zoom_level}, socket) do
updated_options = update_zoom_level(socket.assigns.chart_options, zoom_level)
{:noreply, assign(socket, :chart_options, updated_options)}
end
```

For complex dashboards with multiple visualizations, we need to manage resources efficiently. This might involve implementing lazy loading and viewport-based rendering:

```elixir
def handle_event("visibility_changed", %{"visible" => visible, "chart_id" => id}, socket) do
if visible do
send(self(), {:load_chart_data, id})
{:noreply, update(socket, :active_charts, &MapSet.put(&1, id))}
else
{:noreply, update(socket, :active_charts, &MapSet.delete(&1, id))}
end
end
```

Animation and transitions can greatly enhance the user experience, but they need to be implemented carefully to maintain performance:

```javascript
Hooks.AnimatedChart = {
mounted() {
this.chart = new Chart(this.el, {
options: {
animation: {
duration: 750,
easing: 'easeInOutQuart',
onProgress: (animation) => {
this.handleAnimationProgress(animation)
}
}
}
})
```

```
}
}
```

For geographic visualizations, we might need to implement specialized rendering and data processing:

```elixir
def prepare_geo_data(raw_data) do
raw_data
|> Enum.group_by(&{&1.latitude, &1.longitude})
|> Enum.map(fn {{lat, lng}, points} ->
%{
coordinates: [lat, lng],
value: aggregate_geo_points(points),
weight: length(points)
}
end)
end
```

Performance optimization becomes crucial when dealing with real-time visualizations. We can implement various strategies to maintain responsiveness:

```elixir
defmodule MyApp.VisualizationOptimizer do
def optimize_dataset(data, target_points) do
data_length = length(data)
if data_length > target_points do
reduction_factor = div(data_length, target_points)
data
|> Enum.chunk_every(reduction_factor)
|> Enum.map(&aggregate_chunk/1)
else
data
```

```
end
end
end
```

By carefully implementing these visualization patterns and considering both performance and user experience, we can create compelling real-time visualizations that scale well and provide valuable insights to users. The key is to balance update frequency, data processing, and rendering capabilities while maintaining system responsiveness and data accuracy.

# 16. WebSocket Authentication

In this chapter, we'll explore the crucial aspects of WebSocket authentication in Phoenix applications. Authentication is a fundamental security requirement for real-time applications, ensuring that only authorized users can establish WebSocket connections and access protected resources.

WebSocket authentication in Phoenix typically occurs during the initial connection phase. Unlike traditional HTTP requests where authentication can be handled on a per-request basis, WebSocket connections require authentication to be validated during the initial handshake, as the connection will persist afterward.

Let's start with implementing a basic authentication system for WebSocket connections. In Phoenix, we can leverage the socket connection phase to perform authentication:

```elixir
defmodule MyAppWeb.UserSocket do
use Phoenix.Socket
def connect(%{"token" => token}, socket, _connect_info) do
case verify_token(token) do
{:ok, user_id} ->
{:ok, assign(socket, :user_id, user_id)}
{:error, _reason} ->
:error
end
end
def connect(_params, _socket, _connect_info), do: :error
defp verify_token(token) do
MyApp.TokenAuthenticator.verify(token)
end
end
```

Token-based authentication is particularly well-suited for WebSocket connections. When implementing token authentication, we need to consider token generation, verification, and expiration handling:

```elixir
defmodule MyApp.TokenAuthenticator do
@secret_key Application.compile_env(:my_app, :secret_key)
@token_validity_period 86400 # 24 hours in seconds
def generate_token(user_id) do
Phoenix.Token.sign(@secret_key, "user socket", user_id)
end
def verify_token(token) do
Phoenix.Token.verify(@secret_key, "user socket", token, max_age: @token_validity_period)
end
end
```

Client-side implementation is equally important. We need to ensure the authentication token is properly passed during the WebSocket connection establishment:

```javascript
let socket = new Socket("/socket", {
params: {token: window.userToken}
})
socket.connect()
```

For LiveView applications, authentication can be integrated with the existing session-based authentication system. We can modify the LiveView socket to handle authentication:

```elixir
defmodule MyAppWeb.LiveSocket do
use Phoenix.LiveView.Socket,
```

```
on_mount: {MyAppWeb.LiveAuth, :ensure_authenticated}
end
defmodule MyAppWeb.LiveAuth do
import Phoenix.LiveView
import Phoenix.Component
def on_mount(:ensure_authenticated, _params, session, socket) do
case session do
%{"user_token" => token} ->
case MyApp.TokenAuthenticator.verify_token(token) do
{:ok, user_id} ->
user = MyApp.Accounts.get_user!(user_id)
{:cont, assign(socket, :current_user, user)}
{:error, _} ->
{:halt, redirect(socket, to: "/login")}
end
_ ->
{:halt, redirect(socket, to: "/login")}
end
end
end
```

When dealing with multiple authentication methods, we might need to implement a more flexible authentication system:

```elixir
defmodule MyApp.Authentication do
def authenticate_socket(params) do
cond do
token = params["token"] ->
authenticate_token(token)
api_key = params["api_key"] ->
authenticate_api_key(api_key)
```

```
true ->
{:error, :invalid_credentials}
end
end
defp authenticate_token(token) do
case MyApp.TokenAuthenticator.verify_token(token) do
{:ok, user_id} -> {:ok, :token, user_id}
{:error, reason} -> {:error, reason}
end
end
defp authenticate_api_key(api_key) do
case MyApp.ApiKeyStore.verify_key(api_key) do
{:ok, client_id} -> {:ok, :api_key, client_id}
{:error, reason} -> {:error, reason}
end
end
end
```

For enhanced security, we might want to implement rate limiting during the authentication phase:

```elixir
defmodule MyApp.AuthenticationRateLimiter do
use GenServer
def check_rate(ip_address) do
case :ets.update_counter(:auth_attempts, ip_address, {2, 1}, {ip_address, 0}) do
count when count > 5 ->
{:error, :rate_limited}
_count ->
:ok
end
end
```

```
def init(_) do
:ets.new(:auth_attempts, [:named_table, :set, :public])
schedule_cleanup()
{:ok, %{}}
end
defp schedule_cleanup do
Process.send_after(self(), :cleanup, 60_000)
end
def handle_info(:cleanup, state) do
:ets.delete_all_objects(:auth_attempts)
schedule_cleanup()
{:noreply, state}
end
end
```

When implementing authentication for distributed systems, we need to consider how authentication state is shared across nodes:

```elixir
defmodule MyApp.DistributedAuthCache do
def store_session(session_id, user_id) do
:erpc.multicall(Node.list(), __MODULE__, :do_store_session, [session_id, user_id])
end
def verify_session(session_id) do
case :ets.lookup(:session_cache, session_id) do
[{^session_id, user_id}] -> {:ok, user_id}
[] -> {:error, :session_not_found}
end
end
def do_store_session(session_id, user_id) do
:ets.insert(:session_cache, {session_id, user_id})
end
```

```
end
```

Finally, it's important to implement proper logging and monitoring for authentication events.

```elixir
defmodule MyApp.AuthenticationLogger do
require Logger
def log_authentication_attempt(result, metadata) do
case result do
{:ok, user_id} ->
Logger.info("Successful authentication",
user_id: user_id,
ip_address: metadata.ip_address,
timestamp: DateTime.utc_now()
)
{:error, reason} ->
Logger.warn("Failed authentication attempt",
reason: reason,
ip_address: metadata.ip_address,
timestamp: DateTime.utc_now()
)
end
end
end
```

By implementing these authentication patterns and security measures, we can ensure that our WebSocket connections are properly secured while maintaining scalability and performance. Remember to regularly review and update security measures as new threats emerge and best practices evolve.

# 17. Channel Authorization

Channel authorization is a critical security component in real-time Phoenix applications. Without proper authorization, malicious users could join any channel, listen to private conversations, or send unauthorized messages. In this chapter, we'll explore how to implement robust authorization for Phoenix Channels, ensuring that users can only access the resources they're permitted to see.

Authorization in Phoenix Channels happens at two key moments: when a user attempts to join a channel and when they try to send messages through an established connection. The join authorization occurs in the socket's connect/3 callback and the channel's join/3 function, while ongoing message authorization happens in handle_in/3. This layered approach provides defense in depth, ensuring security at multiple levels.

Let's start with socket connections. When a client attempts to establish a WebSocket connection, Phoenix first calls the socket's connect/3 callback. This is our first line of defense, where we verify the user's authentication token and establish their identity. A common pattern is to decode a JWT token provided in the connection parameters, verify its signature, and load the corresponding user record from the database.

Socket authentication requires careful handling of failure cases. If authentication fails, we must immediately reject the connection attempt. However, we should be cautious about error messages – providing too much detail about why authentication failed could help attackers probe our system. Instead, we return generic error messages that don't reveal internal implementation details.

Once the socket connection is authenticated, users still need authorization to join specific channels. The join/3 callback in each channel module provides fine-grained control over channel access.

Here, we can implement complex authorization rules based on the user's roles, permissions, or relationship to the requested resource. For example, in a chat application, we might verify that the user is a member of the requested chat room before allowing them to join the channel.

Proper error handling during channel joins is crucial for security and user experience. When denying access, we should return clear but secure error messages that help legitimate users understand why their request was denied without revealing sensitive information. We implement standardized error responses that maintain security while providing actionable feedback.

Authorization doesn't stop after the initial join. Every incoming message must be authorized before processing. The handle_in/3 callback provides a hook for implementing per-message authorization rules. Here, we can verify that the user has permission to perform specific actions within the channel. For example, in a moderated chat room, we might check if the user has moderator privileges before allowing them to delete messages.

Rate limiting is an important aspect of channel authorization. Even authorized users shouldn't be allowed to flood channels with messages or perform actions too frequently. We implement rate limiting at both the socket and channel levels, using token buckets or sliding windows to enforce fair usage policies. This prevents denial of service attacks while ensuring good user experience for legitimate users.

To support complex authorization rules, we often need to maintain additional state. Phoenix Channels provides several options for state management. The socket assigns map stores user-specific data available throughout the connection lifecycle. Channel-specific state can be stored in the channel's state map. For more complex scenarios, we can use Phoenix PubSub to coordinate authorization state across multiple nodes.

Role-based authorization adds another layer of complexity. Users might have different roles in different contexts – for example, being a moderator in one chat room but a regular user in another. We implement a flexible role system that can handle these varying permissions, storing role information in a way that's efficiently accessible during authorization checks.

Authorization rules often need to consider resource ownership. In our chat application, message authors might have special privileges to edit or delete their own messages. We implement ownership checks that compare the current user's identity with resource ownership records, ensuring users can only modify their own content while allowing administrators to override these restrictions when necessary.

Auditing is crucial for security monitoring and compliance. We implement comprehensive logging of authorization decisions, recording who attempted to access what resources and whether access was granted or denied. These audit logs help us detect potential security breaches and provide accountability for administrative actions.

Testing authorization logic requires careful consideration. We write tests that verify both successful and failed authorization attempts, ensuring our system correctly handles edge cases. Mock users with different permission levels help us verify that our authorization rules work correctly across various scenarios. We also implement integration tests that verify authorization works correctly across the entire system.

When authorization rules change, we need to handle existing connections gracefully. We implement a system for pushing authorization updates to connected clients, allowing us to revoke access or grant new permissions without requiring users to reconnect. This dynamic authorization system provides flexibility while maintaining security.

Finally, we consider authorization in the context of distributed systems. When running multiple Phoenix nodes, authorization state needs to remain consistent across the cluster. We use Phoenix PubSub to broadcast authorization changes and implement appropriate caching strategies to maintain performance while ensuring security isn't compromised by stale authorization data.

Through these implementations, we create a robust, flexible authorization system that provides strong security while remaining maintainable and performant. By carefully considering authentication, authorization, and auditing at each level, we ensure our real-time features are both powerful and secure.

# 18. Managing WebSocket Connections

Managing WebSocket connections at scale presents unique challenges. Unlike traditional HTTP requests that follow a request-response cycle, WebSocket connections persist indefinitely, maintaining bi-directional communication between client and server. In this chapter, we'll explore strategies for efficiently managing these long-lived connections in Phoenix applications.

• • • •

AT ITS CORE, EACH WEBSOCKET connection in Phoenix is backed by an Erlang process. This process-per-connection model is one of Elixir's key strengths, allowing applications to handle thousands or even millions of concurrent connections efficiently. However, this power comes with responsibility – we need to carefully manage these connections to prevent resource leaks and ensure optimal performance.

• • • •

CONNECTION LIFECYCLE management starts with the socket connection phase. When a client initiates a WebSocket connection, Phoenix calls the connect/3 callback in our socket module. This is where we perform initial setup, authenticate the user, and allocate any necessary resources. It's crucial to keep this phase lightweight – any slow operations here will impact connection establishment latency for all clients.

• • • •

RESOURCE CLEANUP IS a critical consideration when managing WebSocket connections. Every connection consumes memory and may hold references to other resources like database connections or external API tokens. The terminate/2 callback provides a hook for cleaning up these resources when connections close. We implement comprehensive cleanup routines that release all allocated resources, preventing memory leaks that could accumulate over time.

• • • •

CONNECTION MONITORING helps us understand the health of our system. We implement telemetry hooks that track key metrics like connection duration, message frequency, and payload sizes. These metrics help us identify problematic patterns – for example, connections that send unusually large messages or clients that repeatedly disconnect and reconnect. By monitoring these patterns, we can detect and address issues before they impact system stability.

• • • •

HANDLING DISCONNECTIONS gracefully is essential for a good user experience. Network issues can cause temporary disconnections, and clients might close their browsers without properly terminating connections. We implement heartbeat mechanisms that detect stale connections and clean them up automatically. When clients reconnect, we restore their previous state and replay any missed messages to maintain consistency.

• • • •

CONNECTION POOLING becomes important when dealing with external resources. While each WebSocket connection has its own process, we don't want each one maintaining its own database connection or external API client. Instead, we implement connection pools that are shared across WebSocket connections, using tools like poolboy to manage these shared resources efficiently.

• • • •

MESSAGE QUEUING HELPS handle bursts of activity. When many clients send messages simultaneously, we queue messages for processing rather than handling them all immediately. This prevents resource exhaustion during peak loads while ensuring all messages are processed eventually. We implement prioritization schemes that handle important messages (like system notifications) before processing less critical updates.

• • • •

RATE LIMITING IS CRUCIAL for protecting server resources. We implement token bucket algorithms that limit how frequently individual clients can send messages. This prevents aggressive clients from overwhelming the system while allowing occasional bursts of activity. The rate limiting system scales with the application, adjusting limits based on server load and available resources.

• • • •

CONNECTION STATE MANAGEMENT requires careful consideration. While Phoenix provides mechanism for storing state in socket assigns, keeping too much state in memory can impact performance. We implement strategies for persisting state to databases or caches when necessary, while keeping frequently accessed data in memory for performance.

• • • •

SCALING WEBSOCKET CONNECTIONS across multiple nodes introduces additional complexity. We use Phoenix PubSub to coordinate between nodes, ensuring messages reach all relevant clients regardless of which node they're connected to. The distributed nature of Elixir helps here, as messages can be efficiently routed between nodes without requiring complex external message brokers.

• • • •

ERROR HANDLING IN WEBSOCKET connections must be robust. Unlike HTTP requests where errors affect only a single request, WebSocket errors can impact long-lived connections. We implement comprehensive error handling that catches and logs errors while preventing them from crashing the connection process. This includes handling both expected errors (like invalid message formats) and unexpected exceptions.

• • • •

MEMORY MANAGEMENT BECOMES critical at scale. Each WebSocket connection maintains some state in memory, and this can add up with thousands of connections. We implement memory monitoring that tracks per-connection memory usage and implements strategies for reducing memory pressure when needed. This might include garbage collecting unused state or disconnecting idle clients during high-load situations.

• • • •

LOAD BALANCING WEBSOCKET connections requires special consideration. Unlike HTTP requests, WebSocket connections must maintain affinity to specific servers. We implement consistent hashing strategies that distribute connections across nodes while ensuring reconnecting clients return to the same node when possible. This helps maintain session consistency while balancing load across the cluster.

• • • •

CONNECTION SECURITY remains important throughout the connection lifecycle. We implement periodic token validation to ensure connections remain authorized, and monitor for suspicious patterns that might indicate security threats. This includes detecting attempts to spam connections or abuse system resources.

• • • •

FINALLY, WE IMPLEMENT graceful shutdown procedures for maintenance or deployments. When a node needs to be taken down, we notify connected clients and give them time to reconnect to other nodes. This prevents service interruptions during routine maintenance while ensuring all connections are properly closed and resources are cleaned up.

• • • •

THROUGH THESE IMPLEMENTATIONS, we create a robust system for managing WebSocket connections at scale. The combination of Elixir's process model and Phoenix's WebSocket abstractions provides a solid foundation, while our careful management ensures reliable operation even under heavy load.

# 19. Handling Connection Drops

In any real-time application, handling connection drops gracefully is crucial for maintaining a positive user experience. Network connections can be unreliable, especially on mobile devices where users frequently move between different networks or experience varying signal strengths. A well-designed application must handle these scenarios elegantly while maintaining data consistency and user state.

When a WebSocket connection drops, several things need to happen simultaneously. First, the client-side application should detect the disconnection and attempt to reconnect automatically. Phoenix provides built-in reconnection logic through its Channel and LiveView implementations, but we can customize this behavior to better suit our application's needs. The default exponential backoff strategy works well in most cases, starting with quick reconnection attempts and gradually increasing the delay between attempts to avoid overwhelming the server.

Let's examine how to implement a robust reconnection strategy. In a Phoenix LiveView application, we can modify the default reconnection behavior by configuring the LiveSocket options:

```javascript
let liveSocket = new LiveSocket("/live", Socket, {
params: {_csrf_token: csrfToken},
reconnectAfterMs: tries => {
return tries * 1000
}
})
```

This simple linear backoff strategy increases the reconnection delay by one second with each attempt. However, for production applications, we typically want more sophisticated handling. We should consider implementing a maximum retry limit, user notifications, and graceful degradation of functionality.

During a connection drop, it's essential to preserve the user's state and any pending changes. For LiveView applications, we can implement a temporary client-side cache that stores important state information. When the connection is reestablished, we can reconcile this cached state with the server state to ensure consistency. This is particularly important for forms and other user inputs where data loss would be frustrating for users.

The server side needs careful consideration as well. When a client disconnects, the associated LiveView process doesn't immediately terminate. Instead, it enters a temporary disconnected state, allowing for potential reconnection. This behavior is configurable through the temporary_assigns option in LiveView:

```elixir
def mount(_params, _session, socket) do
{:ok, socket,
temporary_assigns: [messages: []],
hibernate_after: 5000
}
end
```

This configuration helps manage memory usage during disconnections while maintaining critical state information. The hibernate_after option ensures that inactive processes consume minimal resources while waiting for reconnection.

Error handling during reconnection attempts is crucial. We should implement proper error boundaries and fallback mechanisms. For example, if a LiveView fails to reconnect after several attempts, we might want to redirect the user to a static version of the page or display a meaningful error message with instructions for manual refresh.

Long-running operations deserve special attention when handling connection drops. If a user initiates a significant action just before losing connection, we need strategies to handle the incomplete operation. One approach is to implement idempotent operations where possible, ensuring that retrying the operation won't cause unintended side effects.

For critical applications, implementing a heartbeat mechanism can help detect connection issues before they become apparent to the user. This allows for proactive measures such as saving draft data or warning users about potential connectivity problems:

```elixir
def mount(_params, _session, socket) do
if connected?(socket) do
:timer.send_interval(30000, self(), :heartbeat)
end
{:ok, assign(socket, connection_status: :connected)}
end
def handle_info(:heartbeat, socket) do
{:noreply, socket}
end
```

Mobile applications require additional consideration due to their frequent network transitions. Implementing a progressive enhancement strategy ensures that core functionality remains available even during connection problems. This might involve maintaining a local cache of critical data and implementing offline-first features where appropriate.

When dealing with real-time features like chat or collaborative editing, handling connection drops becomes even more complex. We need to implement message queuing and replay mechanisms to ensure no messages are lost during disconnections. This often involves maintaining a client-side message queue and implementing proper message ordering and deduplication on reconnection.

Database operations during connection drops need careful handling. If a user action requires database updates, we should implement proper transaction handling and rollback mechanisms. Consider using CRDT (Conflict-free Replicated Data Types) for collaborative features where multiple users might be making concurrent changes:

```elixir
defmodule MyApp.CollaborativeDoc do
use Ecto.Schema
schema "collaborative_docs" do
field :content, :string
field :version, :integer
timestamps()
end
def merge_changes(doc, remote_changes) do
# Implement CRDT merge logic
end
end
```

Performance monitoring during reconnection attempts is vital for understanding and improving the user experience. Implement proper logging and metrics collection to track reconnection success rates, timing, and failure patterns. This data helps identify patterns and optimize reconnection strategies:

```elixir
def handle_disconnect(socket) do
Logger.info("Client disconnected",
client_id: socket.assigns.client_id,
timestamp: DateTime.utc_now()
)
```

```
{:ok, socket}
end
```

Finally, consider implementing different reconnection strategies based on the application context. Critical operations might require aggressive reconnection attempts, while background updates could use a more conservative approach. This context-aware handling helps balance server load with user experience requirements.

Remember that connection drops are inevitable in distributed systems. The goal isn't to eliminate them entirely but to handle them gracefully while maintaining data consistency and user experience. Regular testing of disconnection scenarios, including automated tests simulating various network conditions, helps ensure robust handling of these situations in production environments.

# 20. Rate Limiting and Throttling

Rate limiting and throttling are essential aspects of building scalable real-time applications. Without proper controls in place, a system can quickly become overwhelmed by excessive client connections, message volumes, or malicious activity. In this chapter, we'll explore various strategies for implementing rate limiting and throttling in Phoenix applications.

At its core, rate limiting restricts the number of operations a client can perform within a specific time window. This could apply to WebSocket connections, channel messages, LiveView events, or any other interaction with your application. The most basic form of rate limiting tracks request counts within time windows, but sophisticated implementations consider multiple factors like user roles, resource costs, and system load.

Let's start with implementing a simple rate limiter using ETS (Erlang Term Storage) to track message counts. ETS provides an efficient in-memory storage solution that's perfect for rate limiting:

```elixir
defmodule MyApp.RateLimiter do
@table_name :rate_limiter
@max_messages 100
@window_seconds 60
def init do
:ets.new(@table_name, [:set, :named_table, :public])
end
def allow_message?(user_id) do
now = System.system_time(:second)
case :ets.lookup(@table_name, user_id) do
[{^user_id, count, window_start}] when now - window_start >= @window_seconds ->
:ets.insert(@table_name, {user_id, 1, now})
```

```
true
[{^user_id, count, _window_start}] when count >= @max_messages ->
false
[{^user_id, count, window_start}] ->
:ets.insert(@table_name, {user_id, count + 1, window_start})
true
[] ->
:ets.insert(@table_name, {user_id, 1, now})
true
end
end
end
```

For more distributed systems, you might want to use Redis instead of ETS, especially when running multiple nodes. Redis provides atomic operations that make implementing rate limiting straightforward and consistent across your cluster.

Throttling differs slightly from rate limiting in that it focuses on controlling the rate of resource consumption rather than simply counting requests. This becomes particularly important when dealing with real-time features that could generate significant load, like live updates or streaming data.

In Phoenix channels, we can implement throttling at the socket level by controlling message processing rates:

```elixir
defmodule MyApp.UserSocket do
use Phoenix.Socket
channel "room:*", MyApp.RoomChannel
def connect(%{"token" => token}, socket, _connect_info) do
case verify_token(token) do
{:ok, user_id} ->
```

```
socket = assign(socket, :throttle, %{
last_message: System.monotonic_time(:millisecond),
minimum_interval: 100 # Minimum 100ms between messages
})
{:ok, assign(socket, :user_id, user_id)}
{:error, _} ->
:error
end
end
end
```

Then in your channel, you can enforce this throttling:

```elixir
defmodule MyApp.RoomChannel do
use Phoenix.Channel
def handle_in(event, payload, socket) do
case check_throttle(socket) do
{:ok, socket} ->
# Process the message normally
{:reply, {:ok, payload}, socket}
{:throttled, socket} ->
{:reply, {:error, %{reason: "Message rate exceeded"}}, socket}
end
end
defp check_throttle(socket) do
now = System.monotonic_time(:millisecond)
last = socket.assigns.throttle.last_message
min_interval = socket.assigns.throttle.minimum_interval
if now - last >= min_interval do
{:ok, assign(socket, :throttle, %{socket.assigns.throttle | last_message: now})}
else
```

```
{:throttled, socket}
end
end
end
```

For LiveView applications, we might want to implement rate limiting on event handling. This prevents clients from overwhelming the server with rapid-fire events:

```elixir
defmodule MyApp.LiveRateLimiter do
use Phoenix.Component
def on_mount(:default, _params, _session, socket) do
{:cont, assign(socket,
event_timestamp: System.monotonic_time(:millisecond),
event_count: 0
)}
end
def handle_event(event, params, socket) do
case check_rate_limit(socket) do
{:ok, socket} ->
super(event, params, socket)
{:error, socket} ->
{:noreply, put_flash(socket, :error, "Please slow down")}
end
end
end
```

For more sophisticated rate limiting, consider implementing token bucket algorithms. This approach provides more flexibility in handling burst traffic while maintaining overall rate limits:

```elixir
defmodule MyApp.TokenBucket do
```

```
use GenServer
def start_link(opts) do
GenServer.start_link(__MODULE__, opts, name: __MODULE__)
end
def init(opts) do
capacity = Keyword.get(opts, :capacity, 100)
refill_rate = Keyword.get(opts, :refill_rate, 10)
state = %{
capacity: capacity,
tokens: capacity,
refill_rate: refill_rate,
last_refill: System.monotonic_time(:second)
}
{:ok, state}
end
def take_token do
GenServer.call(__MODULE__, :take_token)
end
def handle_call(:take_token, _from, state) do
state = refill_tokens(state)
if state.tokens > 0 do
{:reply, :ok, %{state | tokens: state.tokens - 1}}
else
{:reply, :error, state}
end
end
defp refill_tokens(state) do
now = System.monotonic_time(:second)
elapsed = now - state.last_refill
new_tokens = min(
state.capacity,
```

```
state.tokens + elapsed * state.refill_rate
)
%{state |
tokens: new_tokens,
last_refill: now
}
end
end
```

When implementing rate limiting and throttling, it's crucial to provide clear feedback to users when they hit limits. This might include updating the UI to show remaining quota, implementing progressive backoff for reconnection attempts, or suggesting alternative actions when limits are reached.

Remember to monitor and adjust your rate limiting parameters based on real-world usage patterns. What seems like a reasonable limit during development might prove too restrictive or too lenient in production. Implement proper logging and metrics collection to help tune these values over time.

Finally, consider implementing different rate limiting tiers based on user roles or subscription levels. This allows you to provide better service to premium users while still protecting your system from abuse. Store these configurations in a way that allows easy updates without requiring application restarts.

Rate limiting and throttling are essential tools for building resilient real-time applications. When implemented thoughtfully, they protect your system from overload while maintaining a positive user experience for legitimate users.

# 21. Introduction to OTP Principles

Introduction to OTP Principles marks a crucial turning point in our exploration of real time Phoenix applications. The Open Telecom Platform (OTP) forms the bedrock of Elixir's powerful concurrency and fault tolerance capabilities, providing battle tested abstractions that enable developers to build robust, scalable systems.

At its core, OTP is a set of libraries and design principles that emerged from Ericsson's telecommunications work, where systems needed to handle millions of concurrent connections while maintaining exceptional uptime. These same principles make OTP perfect for modern real time web applications that face similar scalability and reliability challenges.

The fundamental building block of OTP is the process. Unlike operating system processes, Elixir processes are lightweight, allowing applications to spawn millions of them without significant overhead. These processes are completely isolated from each other, communicating only through message passing. This isolation is crucial for fault tolerance as it prevents errors in one process from cascading through the entire system.

Let's explore how processes work by creating a simple counter:

```elixir
defmodule Counter do
def start do
spawn(fn -> loop(0) end)
end
defp loop(count) do
receive do
{:increment} ->
loop(count + 1)
{:get, caller} ->
send(caller, count)
```

```
loop(count)
end
end
end
```

While this example demonstrates basic process principles, it lacks many features we'd want in a production system. How do we handle crashes? What if we want to name our process? How do we manage process state? This is where OTP behaviors come in.

OTP behaviors provide standardized patterns for common programming needs. The most frequently used behaviors include GenServer (for general purpose server processes), Supervisor (for process monitoring and restart strategies), and Application (for packaging and structuring applications).

These behaviors handle the boilerplate of process management, letting developers focus on business logic. They provide consistent patterns for handling initialization, state management, synchronous and asynchronous calls, process termination, and error handling.

Another crucial OTP principle is the "let it crash" philosophy. Rather than trying to anticipate and handle every possible error condition, OTP encourages developers to let processes fail and rely on supervisors to restart them in a clean state. This approach leads to more reliable systems as it's easier to handle failure than to prevent every possible error.

The supervision tree is a fundamental OTP concept that implements this philosophy. Supervisors monitor their child processes and restart them according to predefined strategies when they fail. This creates a hierarchical process structure where failures are isolated and handled at the appropriate level.

Consider this example of a supervision tree for a chat application:

```elixir
```

```
defmodule Chat.Application do
use Application
def start(_type, _args) do
children = [
{Phoenix.PubSub, name: Chat.PubSub},
Chat.Presence,
{DynamicSupervisor, name: Chat.RoomSupervisor, strategy: :one_for_one},
ChatWeb.Endpoint
]
opts = [strategy: :one_for_one, name: Chat.Supervisor]
Supervisor.start_link(children, opts)
end
end
```

OTP also provides tools for building distributed systems. The distribution capabilities are built into the platform, allowing processes to communicate seamlessly across network boundaries. This becomes particularly important when scaling real time applications across multiple nodes.

Error handling in OTP follows structured patterns. The "let it crash" philosophy doesn't mean we ignore errors it means we handle them at the appropriate level. OTP provides mechanisms like monitors and links to track process relationships and handle failures appropriately.

Process monitoring allows one process to be notified when another terminates:

```elixir
def monitor_example do
pid = spawn(fn -> Process.sleep(1000) end)
ref = Process.monitor(pid)
receive do
```

```
{:DOWN, ^ref, :process, ^pid, reason} ->
IO.puts "Process terminated: #{inspect(reason)}"
end
end
```

Links create stronger relationships between processes if one linked process crashes, all processes linked to it will also crash unless they're trapping exits:

```elixir
def link_example do
Process.flag(:trap_exit, true)
pid = spawn_link(fn -> raise "boom" end)
receive do
{:EXIT, ^pid, reason} ->
IO.puts "Linked process crashed: #{inspect(reason)}"
end
end
```

Understanding OTP principles is crucial for building robust real time applications. The standardized behaviors, supervision strategies, and error handling patterns provide a solid foundation for handling the complexities of concurrent systems.

When building Phoenix applications, you'll frequently interact with OTP concepts. Phoenix channels are implemented using GenServers, your application supervision tree manages critical processes, and the PubSub system relies on OTP principles for distribution and fault tolerance.

As we progress through more advanced topics, we'll see how these OTP principles enable features like hot code swapping, system observation, and fault tolerance. The initial investment in understanding OTP concepts pays dividends when building and maintaining production systems.

Remember that OTP isn't just a library it's a philosophy for building reliable distributed systems. The principles of process isolation, supervised process trees, and standardized behaviors have been proven in production systems handling millions of concurrent users. As you build real time features, keep these principles in mind to create systems that are not just functional, but also maintainable and reliable.

# 22. Supervisors and Process Trees

Building upon our introduction to OTP principles, let's dive deep into supervisors and process trees, two fundamental concepts that form the backbone of fault tolerant Elixir applications. Supervisors are specialized processes that monitor other processes, known as child processes, and handle their lifecycle according to predefined strategies.

The primary responsibility of a supervisor is to start, monitor, and restart its child processes when they crash. This creates a hierarchical structure known as a supervision tree, where each supervisor can oversee multiple workers or other supervisors. This hierarchy is crucial for isolating failures and maintaining system stability.

Let's examine the basic structure of a supervisor:

```elixir
defmodule MyApp.Supervisor do
use Supervisor
def start_link(init_arg) do
Supervisor.start_link(__MODULE__, init_arg, name: __MODULE__)
end
@impl true
def init(_init_arg) do
children = [
{MyApp.Worker, []},
{MyApp.Cache, []},
{MyApp.MessageHandler, []}
]
Supervisor.init(children, strategy: :one_for_one)
end
end
```

Supervisors support several restart strategies that determine how child processes are handled when failures occur. The most common strategies are:

:one_for_one - When a child process crashes, only that process is restarted. This is the most commonly used strategy and is suitable when child processes are independent of each other.

:one_for_all - When any child process crashes, all other child processes are terminated and restarted. This strategy is useful when all children need to work together and cannot function independently.

:rest_for_one - When a child process crashes, the failed process and all processes started after it are terminated and restarted. This is helpful when you have dependencies between processes that must be started in a specific order.

The supervision tree typically starts at the application level. When you create a new Phoenix application, it automatically generates an application supervisor that serves as the root of your supervision tree:

```elixir
defmodule MyApp.Application do
use Application
def start(_type, _args) do
children = [
MyApp.Repo,
{Phoenix.PubSub, name: MyApp.PubSub},
MyAppWeb.Endpoint,
{DynamicSupervisor, name: MyApp.DynamicSupervisor}
]
opts = [strategy: :one_for_one, name: MyApp.Supervisor]
Supervisor.start_link(children, opts)
end
```

```
end
```

Dynamic supervision is another powerful feature that allows you to add and remove child processes at runtime. This is particularly useful in real time applications where you might need to create processes for each user connection or chat room:

```elixir
defmodule MyApp.ChatRoom do
def start_room(room_id) do
DynamicSupervisor.start_child(MyApp.DynamicSupervisor, {MyApp.Room, room_id})
end
def stop_room(pid) do
DynamicSupervisor.terminate_child(MyApp.DynamicSupervisor, pid)
end
end
```

Supervisors also support child specification options that provide fine grained control over process management. These options include:

:restart - Defines when the child should be restarted (:permanent, :temporary, or :transient)

:shutdown - Specifies how long to wait for a child to stop before forcefully terminating it

:type - Indicates whether the child is a :worker or :supervisor

Here's an example with detailed child specifications:

```elixir
def init(_init_arg) do
children = [
%{
id: MyApp.Worker,
```

```
start: {MyApp.Worker, :start_link, []},
restart: :permanent,
shutdown: 5000,
type: :worker
}
]
Supervisor.init(children, strategy: :one_for_one)
end
```

When building real time applications, proper supervision tree design is crucial. Consider a WebSocket connection handling system:

```elixir
defmodule MyApp.ConnectionSupervisor do
use Supervisor
def start_link(init_arg) do
Supervisor.start_link(__MODULE__, init_arg, name: __MODULE__)
end
def init(_init_arg) do
children = [
{Registry, keys: :unique, name: MyApp.ConnectionRegistry},
{DynamicSupervisor, name: MyApp.ConnectionHandler, strategy: :one_for_one}
]
Supervisor.init(children, strategy: :one_for_one)
end
end
```

This supervisor manages a registry for tracking connections and a dynamic supervisor for handling individual connection processes.

The separation of concerns and proper hierarchy ensure that failures in individual connections don't affect the entire system.

Process trees should be designed with careful consideration of process relationships and failure modes. When processes have dependencies, they should be grouped under appropriate supervisors with suitable restart strategies. For example, if you have a cache process that depends on a database connection, they might be supervised together with a :rest_for_one strategy.

Monitoring the health of your supervision tree is essential in production environments. The Observer tool, built into the Erlang runtime, provides valuable insights into your process tree structure and runtime behavior:

```elixir
:observer.start()
```

Remember that supervisors themselves are processes and can be supervised by other supervisors. This creates a hierarchical structure that can handle failures at any level of your application. The key is to design your supervision tree to match the natural hierarchy and dependencies of your system components.

In real time applications, proper supervisor design becomes especially important when handling features like presence tracking, channel management, and connection pooling. Each of these components might require its own supervision subtree to manage its specific failure modes and recovery strategies.

As your application grows, you might need to adjust your supervision strategies and process organization. Always consider the impact of process failures and how they should be handled in your specific use case. The goal is to create a system that can recover from failures automatically and maintain stability even under unexpected conditions.

Through careful supervision tree design and proper use of restart strategies, you can build real time applications that are resilient and self healing. The supervision mechanisms provided by OTP handle the complex details of process management, allowing you to focus on building features while maintaining system reliability.

# 23. GenServers in Real-Time Applications

GenServers form the cornerstone of state management and concurrency in real time Elixir applications. Building on our understanding of supervisors and process trees, we'll explore how GenServers enable robust, stateful processes that can handle concurrent operations efficiently.

A GenServer is a behavior module that implements a client server relationship where a process maintains state and handles various types of requests. In real time applications, GenServers are particularly valuable for managing shared state, handling long running operations, and coordinating between multiple clients.

Let's start with a basic example of a GenServer that manages a chat room's state:

```elixir
defmodule ChatRoom do
use GenServer
def start_link(room_name) do
GenServer.start_link(__MODULE__, room_name, name: via_tuple(room_name))
end
def init(room_name) do
{:ok, %{name: room_name, messages: [], participants: MapSet.new()}}
end
def add_message(room_name, message) do
GenServer.call(via_tuple(room_name), {:add_message, message})
end
def get_messages(room_name) do
GenServer.call(via_tuple(room_name), :get_messages)
end
```

```elixir
def handle_call({:add_message, message}, _from, state) do
new_messages = [message | state.messages]
new_state = %{state | messages: new_messages}
{:reply, :ok, new_state}
end
def handle_call(:get_messages, _from, state) do
{:reply, Enum.reverse(state.messages), state}
end
defp via_tuple(room_name) do
{:via, Registry, {ChatRegistry, room_name}}
end
end
```

In real time applications, GenServers often need to handle asynchronous operations. The handle_cast callback is perfect for these scenarios, as it doesn't block the caller:

```elixir
def broadcast_message(room_name, message) do
GenServer.cast(via_tuple(room_name), {:broadcast, message})
end
def handle_cast({:broadcast, message}, state) do
Phoenix.PubSub.broadcast(MyApp.PubSub,
"room:#{state.name}", {:new_message, message})
{:noreply, state}
end
```

GenServers also support periodic or scheduled work through handle_info callbacks. This is particularly useful for cleanup tasks or periodic state updates:

```elixir
def init(room_name) do
schedule_cleanup()
```

```
{:ok, %{name: room_name, messages: [], participants: MapSet.new()}}
end
def handle_info(:cleanup, state) do
schedule_cleanup()
old_messages = Enum.filter(state.messages, &message_within_timeframe?/1)
{:noreply, %{state | messages: old_messages}}
end
defp schedule_cleanup do
Process.send_after(self(), :cleanup, :timer.hours(24))
end
```

When building real time applications, it's crucial to consider message handling timeouts. GenServer calls can specify timeouts to prevent indefinite waiting:

```elixir
def get_messages_with_timeout(room_name) do
GenServer.call(via_tuple(room_name), :get_messages, 5000)
rescue
exit(:timeout) -> {:error, :timeout}
end
```

State management becomes more complex when dealing with concurrent operations. GenServers handle this naturally by processing messages sequentially:

```elixir
def handle_call({:join_room, user}, _from, state) do
if MapSet.member?(state.participants, user) do
{:reply, {:error, :already_joined}, state}
else
new_participants = MapSet.put(state.participants, user)
```

```
{:reply, :ok, %{state | participants: new_participants}}
end
end
```

For real time applications handling many connections, it's important to implement proper termination handling:

```elixir
def terminate(reason, state) do
Logger.info("ChatRoom #{state.name} terminating due to #{inspect(reason)}")
Phoenix.PubSub.broadcast(MyApp.PubSub, "room:#{state.name}", :room_closed)
:ok
end
```

When building scalable applications, you might need to implement GenServers that can handle backpressure:

```elixir
def handle_call({:add_message, message}, from, state) when length(state.messages) >= 1000 do
Process.send_after(self(), {:retry_add_message, message, from}, 1000)
{:noreply, state}
end
def handle_info({:retry_add_message, message, from}, state) do
if length(state.messages) < 1000 do
new_messages = [message | state.messages]
GenServer.reply(from, :ok)
{:noreply, %{state | messages: new_messages}}
else
Process.send_after(self(), {:retry_add_message, message, from}, 1000)
```

{:noreply, state}
end
end
```

GenServers can also implement the handle_continue callback for performing expensive initialization after returning from init:

```elixir
def init(room_name) do
{:ok, %{name: room_name}, {:continue, :load_history}}
end
def handle_continue(:load_history, state) do
messages = Database.load_room_history(state.name)
{:noreply, %{state | messages: messages}}
end
```

For real time applications requiring distributed state, GenServers can be enhanced with global registration:

```elixir
def start_link(room_name) do
GenServer.start_link(__MODULE__, room_name, name: {:global, {__MODULE__, room_name}})
end
def add_message(room_name, message) do
GenServer.call({:global, {__MODULE__, room_name}}, {:add_message, message})
end
```

When implementing GenServers in production applications, it's important to include proper monitoring and metrics:

```elixir
def handle_call(message, from, state) do
start_time = System.monotonic_time()
```
```

```
result = do_handle_call(message, from, state)
duration = System.monotonic_time() - start_time
:telemetry.execute([:chat_room, :call], %{duration: duration},
%{message: message})
result
end
```

GenServers are essential building blocks for real time applications, providing a robust foundation for managing state and handling concurrent operations. By carefully considering message handling, timeouts, and state management, you can build scalable and reliable real time features that maintain consistency even under high load.

Remember that GenServers should be used judiciously. While they excel at managing state and handling concurrent operations, they can become bottlenecks if overused. Consider using them primarily for maintaining important shared state and coordinating between multiple processes, while delegating heavy computational work to separate processes or worker pools.

# 24. Building Fault-Tolerant Systems

Building fault-tolerant systems is a critical aspect of developing reliable real time applications in Elixir. By leveraging OTP principles and Phoenix's built-in capabilities, we can create systems that gracefully handle failures and maintain service availability even when things go wrong.

The foundation of fault tolerance in Elixir applications starts with proper process isolation and supervision. When a process fails, we want to contain that failure and prevent it from cascading through our system. Let's examine a comprehensive approach to building fault tolerance into our real time applications.

First, let's consider how to structure our supervision trees to maximize fault tolerance. Rather than placing all processes under a single supervisor, we should group them based on their failure domains:

```elixir
defmodule MyApp.Application do
use Application
def start(_type, _args) do
children = [
{Phoenix.PubSub, name: MyApp.PubSub},
MyApp.Repo,
{Registry, keys: :unique, name: MyApp.RoomRegistry},
MyApp.RoomSupervisor,
MyApp.UserPresenceSupervisor,
MyApp.MetricsCollector
]
opts = [strategy: :one_for_one, name: MyApp.Supervisor]
Supervisor.start_link(children, opts)
end
end
```

In real time applications, we need to handle various types of failures, from network issues to process crashes. One effective pattern is implementing circuit breakers for external service calls:

```elixir
defmodule MyApp.CircuitBreaker do
use GenServer
def start_link(opts) do
GenServer.start_link(__MODULE__, opts, name: __MODULE__)
end
def check_health(service) do
GenServer.call(__MODULE__, {:check_health, service})
end
def record_failure(service) do
GenServer.cast(__MODULE__, {:record_failure, service})
end
def handle_call({:check_health, service}, _from, state) do
case Map.get(state.failures, service, 0) do
count when count >= state.threshold ->
{:reply, :circuit_open, state}
_ ->
{:reply, :circuit_closed, state}
end
end
end
```

When dealing with WebSocket connections, we need to implement proper error handling and recovery mechanisms. Here's an example of a resilient channel implementation:

```elixir
defmodule MyApp.RoomChannel do
```

```
use Phoenix.Channel
require Logger
def join("room:" <> room_id, _params, socket) do
try do
case MyApp.RoomServer.join_room(room_id, socket.assigns.user_id) do
{:ok, messages} ->
{:ok, %{messages: messages}, socket}
{:error, reason} ->
{:error, %{reason: reason}}
end
rescue
error ->
Logger.error("Failed to join room: #{inspect(error)}")
{:error, %{reason: "internal_error"}}
end
end
end
```

Data consistency is crucial in real time applications. We can implement retry mechanisms with exponential backoff for database operations:

```elixir
defmodule MyApp.Persistence do
def save_with_retry(fun, attempts \\ 3) do
try do
fun.()
rescue
error in [Ecto.StaleEntryError] ->
if attempts > 0 do
Process.sleep(calculate_backoff(attempts))
save_with_retry(fun, attempts - 1)
```

```
else
{:error, :max_retries_reached}
end
end
end
defp calculate_backoff(attempts) do
base = :math.pow(2, 4 - attempts) * 100
trunc(base + :rand.uniform(trunc(base * 0.1)))
end
end
```

Process monitoring is essential for detecting and responding to failures. We can implement a process monitor that tracks critical processes:

```elixir
defmodule MyApp.ProcessMonitor do
use GenServer
def start_link(opts) do
GenServer.start_link(__MODULE__, opts, name: __MODULE__)
end
def monitor_process(pid, metadata) do
GenServer.cast(__MODULE__, {:monitor, pid, metadata})
end
def handle_cast({:monitor, pid, metadata}, state) do
Process.monitor(pid)
{:noreply, Map.put(state, pid, metadata)}
end
def handle_info({:DOWN, _ref, :process, pid, reason}, state) do
metadata = Map.get(state, pid)
handle_process_down(metadata, reason)
{:noreply, Map.delete(state, pid)}
```

```
end
defp handle_process_down(metadata, reason) do
Logger.warn("Process down: #{inspect(metadata)}, reason: #{inspect(reason)}")
notify_administrators(metadata, reason)
attempt_recovery(metadata)
end
end
```

For distributed applications, we need to handle network partitions and split-brain scenarios:

```elixir
defmodule MyApp.ClusterMonitor do
use GenServer
def handle_info({:nodedown, node}, state) do
# Implement partition detection logic
case :global.trans({:cluster_lock, self()},
fn -> check_cluster_status(node) end,
Node.list(),
5000) do
{:ok, :minority} ->
handle_minority_partition()
{:ok, :majority} ->
handle_majority_partition()
{:error, :timeout} ->
handle_uncertain_partition()
end
{:noreply, state}
end
end
```

Error handling should be comprehensive and include proper logging and metrics collection:

```elixir
defmodule MyApp.ErrorHandler do
def handle_error(error, context) do
Logger.error("Error occurred: #{inspect(error)}, context: #{inspect(context)}")
:telemetry.execute(
[:myapp, :error],
%{count: 1},
%{error: error, context: context}
)
case error do
%MyApp.CriticalError{} ->
notify_emergency_contacts(error)
%MyApp.DatabaseError{} ->
attempt_database_recovery()
_ ->
:ok
end
end
end
```

Memory leaks and resource exhaustion can cause system failures. Implementing resource monitoring and automatic cleanup is important:

```elixir
defmodule MyApp.ResourceMonitor do
use GenServer
def init(_) do
schedule_check()
{:ok, %{}}
```

```
end
def handle_info(:check_resources, state) do
memory_usage = :erlang.memory()
process_count = length(Process.list())
if memory_usage[:total] > get_memory_threshold() do
trigger_garbage_collection()
end
if process_count > get_process_threshold() do
terminate_idle_processes()
end
schedule_check()
{:noreply, state}
end
defp schedule_check do
Process.send_after(self(), :check_resources, 60_000)
end
end
```

Building fault-tolerant systems requires careful consideration of failure modes and recovery strategies. By implementing proper supervision trees, error handling, monitoring, and recovery mechanisms, we can create robust real time applications that maintain reliability even under adverse conditions. Remember that fault tolerance is not just about handling errors but about designing systems that can continue operating effectively even when parts of the system fail.

# 25. Distributed Elixir Basics

Distributed computing is one of Elixir's greatest strengths, and the BEAM virtual machine was built from the ground up with distribution in mind. In this chapter, we'll explore the fundamentals of distributed Elixir and how it enables us to build scalable real time applications across multiple nodes.

At its core, distributed Elixir allows multiple Erlang nodes to connect and communicate with each other seamlessly. Each node is a running instance of the BEAM virtual machine, and nodes can be running on the same machine or across different machines in a network. Let's start by understanding how to connect nodes.

To start a named node, we use the—name or—sname flag when starting our application. The difference between them is that—name expects a fully qualified domain name, while—sname uses short names for local networks:

```elixir
iex—name node1@192.168.1.100
# or
iex—sname node1
```

Once we have multiple nodes running, we can connect them using Node.connect/1. When nodes connect, they form a mesh network where each node maintains connections to all other nodes. This is important for building resilient distributed systems:

```elixir
Node.connect(:"node2@192.168.1.101")
Node.list() # Shows all connected nodes
```

One of the most powerful features of distributed Elixir is transparent process communication across nodes. We can spawn processes on remote nodes and send messages between processes regardless of their physical location:

```elixir
# Spawn a process on a remote node
pid = Node.spawn(:"node2@192.168.1.101", fn ->
receive do
{:hello, sender} -> send(sender, {:reply, Node.self()})
end
end)
send(pid, {:hello, self()})
```

When building distributed applications, we need to consider how to handle node connections and disconnections. Here's an example of a module that monitors node connectivity:

```elixir
defmodule MyApp.NodeMonitor do
use GenServer
require Logger
def start_link(opts) do
GenServer.start_link(__MODULE__, opts, name: __MODULE__)
end
def init(_opts) do
:net_kernel.monitor_nodes(true)
{:ok, %{nodes: MapSet.new()}}
end
def handle_info({:nodeup, node}, state) do
Logger.info("Node connected: #{node}")
{:noreply, %{state | nodes: MapSet.put(state.nodes, node)}}
end
def handle_info({:nodedown, node}, state) do
Logger.warn("Node disconnected: #{node}")
```

```
{:noreply, %{state | nodes: MapSet.delete(state.nodes, node)}}
end
end
```

Global registration is another important concept in distributed Elixir. The :global module provides a way to register process names across all connected nodes:

```elixir
defmodule MyApp.GlobalRegistry do
def register_process(name, pid) do
:global.register_name(name, pid)
end
def whereis_name(name) do
:global.whereis_name(name)
end
def send_message(name, message) do
case whereis_name(name) do
:undefined -> {:error, :not_found}
pid -> send(pid, message)
end
end
end
```

Distribution also affects how we handle state in our application. When working with distributed state, we need to consider consistency and partition tolerance. Here's an example of a distributed counter:

```elixir
defmodule MyApp.DistributedCounter do
use GenServer
def start_link(name) do
```

```
GenServer.start_link(__MODULE__, 0, name: {:global, name})
end
def increment(name) do
GenServer.call({:global, name}, :increment)
end
def get_value(name) do
GenServer.call({:global, name}, :get_value)
end
def handle_call(:increment, _from, value) do
{:reply, value + 1, value + 1}
end
def handle_call(:get_value, _from, value) do
{:reply, value, value}
end
end
```

Security is a crucial consideration in distributed systems. By default, Erlang nodes can only connect if they share the same cookie. This cookie acts as a simple authentication mechanism:

```elixir
# Set the cookie when starting the node
iex—name node1@192.168.1.100—cookie secret_cookie
# Or programmatically
Node.set_cookie(Node.self(), :secret_cookie)
```

When building real time applications, we often need to distribute Phoenix PubSub messages across nodes. Phoenix provides built-in support for this through its distributed PubSub adapter:

```elixir
config :my_app, MyApp.PubSub,
adapter: Phoenix.PubSub.PG2,
```

```
pool_size: 1
# In your application.ex
children = [
{Phoenix.PubSub, name: MyApp.PubSub}
]
```

Remote procedure calls (RPC) provide another way to execute code on remote nodes. The :rpc module offers various functions for this purpose:

```elixir
defmodule MyApp.RemoteExecutor do
def execute_on_all_nodes(module, function, args) do
:rpc.multicall(module, function, args)
end
def execute_on_node(node, module, function, args) do
:rpc.call(node, module, function, args)
end
end
```

Understanding how to handle network partitions is essential in distributed systems. Here's a basic implementation of a split-brain detector:

```elixir
defmodule MyApp.PartitionDetector do
use GenServer
def init(_) do
:net_kernel.monitor_nodes(true)
{:ok, %{expected_nodes: Application.get_env(:my_app,
:cluster_nodes)}}
end
def handle_info({:nodedown, node}, state) do
connected_nodes = Node.list()
```

```
expected = state.expected_nodes
if length(connected_nodes) < length(expected) / 2 do
handle_minority_partition()
end
{:noreply, state}
end
defp handle_minority_partition do
# Implement partition handling logic
Logger.warn("Node is in minority partition")
end
end
```

Distributed Elixir provides a powerful foundation for building scalable real time applications. By understanding these basics, you can begin to leverage the full power of distribution in your Phoenix applications. Remember that distributed systems introduce additional complexity, so it's important to carefully consider your architecture and failure modes when building distributed applications.

In the next chapter, we'll dive deeper into node communication patterns and explore more advanced distributed system concepts. We'll look at how to implement reliable message passing, handle network partitions gracefully, and maintain consistency across your distributed system.

# 26. Node Communication

Building upon our understanding of distributed Elixir basics, let's explore the various patterns and techniques for communication between nodes in a distributed system. Node communication is fundamental to building reliable and scalable real time applications.

When nodes in a distributed Elixir system communicate, they do so through message passing. This communication can take several forms, from simple process messages to sophisticated distributed data structures. Let's explore these patterns in detail.

The most basic form of node communication is direct process messaging. While we can send messages between processes on different nodes just like we do locally, we need to consider additional factors such as network latency and potential failures:

```elixir
defmodule MessageRouter do
def send_to_node(node, process_name, message) do
case :global.whereis_name(process_name) do
:undefined ->
{:error, :process_not_found}
pid when node(pid) == node ->
send(pid, message)
{:ok, :sent}
_ ->
{:error, :wrong_node}
end
end
end
```

For more reliable communication patterns, we can implement acknowledgment mechanisms to ensure message delivery:

```elixir
defmodule ReliableMessenger do
def send_and_await(target_pid, message, timeout \\ 5000) do
ref = make_ref()
send(target_pid, {:reliable_msg, self(), ref, message})
receive do
{:ack, ^ref} -> {:ok, :delivered}
after
timeout -> {:error, :timeout}
end
end
end
```

When building distributed applications, we often need to coordinate actions across multiple nodes. The GenServer.multi_call/4 function provides a convenient way to do this:

```elixir
defmodule ClusterCoordinator do
def broadcast_action(action, args) do
GenServer.multi_call(Node.list(), CoordinatorServer, {:action, action, args})
end
def handle_responses({responses, bad_nodes}) do
case bad_nodes do
[] -> {:ok, responses}
failed -> {:partial, responses, failed}
end
end
end
```

For more complex scenarios, we might need to implement custom communication protocols. Here's an example of a three phase commit protocol:

```elixir
defmodule ThreePhaseCommit do
def coordinate_action(nodes, action) do
with {:ok, prepared} <- prepare_phase(nodes, action),
{:ok, committed} <- commit_phase(prepared, action) do
complete_phase(committed, action)
else
{:error, reason} ->
abort_transaction(nodes, action)
{:error, reason}
end
end
defp prepare_phase(nodes, action) do
results = Enum.map(nodes, fn node ->
:rpc.call(node, TransactionHandler, :prepare, [action])
end)
if Enum.all?(results, &match?({:ok, :prepared}, &1)) do
{:ok, nodes}
else
{:error, :preparation_failed}
end
end
end
```

When dealing with large amounts of data between nodes, we need to consider bandwidth and serialization overhead. Here's a pattern for chunked data transfer:

```elixir
defmodule ChunkedTransfer do
```

```
@chunk_size 1024 * 1024 # 1MB chunks
def send_large_data(target_node, data) do
data
|> Stream.chunk_every(@chunk_size)
|> Stream.with_index()
|> Enum.each(fn {chunk, index} ->
:erpc.call(target_node, ChunkReceiver, :receive_chunk, [
chunk,
index,
byte_size(data)
])
end)
end
end
```

Node communication often involves synchronizing state across the cluster. Here's an implementation of a distributed cache with eventual consistency:

```elixir
defmodule DistributedCache do
use GenServer
def put(key, value) do
GenServer.cast(__MODULE__, {:replicate, key, value})
end
def handle_cast({:replicate, key, value}, state) do
:rpc.multicall(Node.list(), __MODULE__, :local_put, [key, value])
{:noreply, Map.put(state, key, value)}
end
def local_put(key, value) do
GenServer.cast(__MODULE__, {:local_put, key, value})
end
```

```
end
```

For real time applications, we often need to implement heartbeat mechanisms to detect node health:

```elixir
defmodule NodeHeartbeat do
use GenServer
@heartbeat_interval 5000
def init(_) do
schedule_heartbeat()
{:ok, %{node_health: %{}}}
end
def handle_info(:heartbeat, state) do
new_health = Node.list()
|> Enum.map(fn node ->
{node, check_node_health(node)}
end)
|> Enum.into(%{})
schedule_heartbeat()
{:noreply, %{state | node_health: new_health}}
end
defp check_node_health(node) do
case :rpc.call(node, :erlang, :date, [], 1000) do
{:badrpc, _} -> :unhealthy
_ -> :healthy
end
end
end
```

When implementing node communication, we need to consider network partitions and split brain scenarios. Here's a pattern for leader election that helps maintain consistency:

```elixir
defmodule LeaderElection do
def elect_leader do
nodes = [Node.self() | Node.list()]
sorted_nodes = Enum.sort(nodes)
case Enum.find_index(sorted_nodes, &(&1 == Node.self()))
do
0 -> {:ok, :leader}
_ -> {:ok, :follower}
end
end
def handle_leader_duties do
case elect_leader() do
{:ok, :leader} ->
coordinate_cluster()
{:ok, :follower} ->
monitor_leader()
end
end
end
```

Communication between nodes should be resilient to failures. Here's a pattern for implementing circuit breakers in node communication:

```elixir
defmodule CircuitBreaker do
def call_protected(node, module, function, args) do
case check_circuit(node) do
:open ->
{:error, :circuit_open}
:closed ->
try do
```

```
result = :rpc.call(node, module, function, args)
record_success(node)
{:ok, result}
catch
_ ->
record_failure(node)
{:error, :call_failed}
end
end
end
end
```

Finally, it's important to implement proper logging and monitoring for node communication. Here's an example of a communication logger:

```elixir
defmodule CommunicationLogger do
require Logger
def log_communication(source_node, target_node, message_type, result) do
metadata = %{
source_node: source_node,
target_node: target_node,
message_type: message_type,
timestamp: DateTime.utc_now(),
result: result
}
Logger.metadata(metadata)
Logger.info("Node communication completed")
end
end
```

Understanding these communication patterns is crucial for building reliable distributed systems. In the next chapter, we'll explore how to maintain consistent state across nodes and handle data synchronization in a distributed environment.

# 27. State Synchronization Across Nodes

State synchronization is one of the most challenging aspects of distributed systems. When running a Phoenix application across multiple nodes, maintaining consistent state becomes crucial for features like real-time updates, presence tracking, and concurrent data access. In this chapter, we'll explore patterns and strategies for keeping state synchronized across a distributed Phoenix cluster.

• • • •

UNDERSTANDING PHOENIX'S distributed architecture is essential for effective state synchronization. Each node in a Phoenix cluster runs independently, maintaining its own Erlang VM and process state. These nodes communicate through Erlang's built-in distribution system, which provides reliable message passing between nodes. However, this distributed nature means we need explicit strategies for keeping state consistent across the cluster.

• • • •

PHOENIX PUBSUB FORMS the foundation of our state synchronization strategy. When state changes occur on one node, we broadcast these changes through PubSub to all other nodes in the cluster. This broadcast mechanism ensures that all nodes receive state updates, but we need careful implementation to handle race conditions, message ordering, and partial failures.

• • • •

THE CAP THEOREM HEAVILY influences our synchronization design choices. In a distributed system, we can't simultaneously guarantee consistency, availability, and partition tolerance. Phoenix applications typically favor availability and partition tolerance, implementing eventual consistency for most state synchronization needs. This means accepting that nodes may temporarily have divergent state, with mechanisms to resolve these differences over time.

• • • •

CRDTS (CONFLICT-FREE Replicated Data Types) play a crucial role in our synchronization strategy. These special data structures are designed to automatically resolve conflicts in distributed systems. Phoenix Presence, which we've discussed in earlier chapters, uses a CRDT implementation for tracking user presence. We can apply similar patterns for other types of state that need automatic conflict resolution.

• • • •

FOR MUTABLE STATE THAT requires stricter consistency, we implement a primary-secondary pattern. One node is designated as the primary for certain state operations, with other nodes forwarding requests to the primary. This ensures sequential consistency for critical operations while maintaining the ability to read state from any node. The trade-off is increased latency for write operations and the need to handle primary node failures.

• • • •

STATE VERSIONING HELPS manage concurrent updates. Each piece of state includes a version number or timestamp that gets incremented with each modification. When nodes exchange state updates, they can use these versions to detect and resolve conflicts. We implement a Lamport clock system that provides a partial ordering of events across the cluster.

• • • •

CACHE SYNCHRONIZATION presents particular challenges in distributed systems. Each node typically maintains its own cache to improve performance, but these caches need to stay reasonably consistent across the cluster. We implement cache invalidation broadcasts that notify all nodes when cached data becomes stale. This approach balances performance with consistency, allowing nodes to maintain independent caches while providing mechanisms for synchronization.

• • • •

HANDLING NODE FAILURES requires careful consideration in our synchronization strategy. When a node goes down, it misses state updates that occur while it's offline. When the node comes back online, it needs to resynchronize its state with the rest of the cluster. We implement a state recovery protocol that allows rejoining nodes to request state updates they missed during downtime.

• • • •

DATABASE-BACKED STATE adds another layer of complexity. While the database provides a source of truth for persistent data, nodes need to synchronize their in-memory state and caches with this persistent storage. We implement optimistic concurrency control using database transactions and version numbers to detect and resolve conflicts between nodes accessing the same data.

• • • •

REAL-TIME COLLABORATION features require particularly sophisticated synchronization. When multiple users are simultaneously editing shared data, we need to maintain consistency while providing responsive updates. We implement Operational Transform algorithms for text editing and similar collaboration features, ensuring that concurrent edits result in consistent final state across all nodes.

• • • •

STATE SEGMENTATION helps manage synchronization overhead. Instead of synchronizing all state across all nodes, we partition state based on usage patterns. States that are frequently accessed together are kept on the same node, reducing the need for cross-node synchronization. This approach improves performance but requires careful design to maintain data locality.

• • • •

BACKGROUND RECONCILIATION helps handle edge cases in state synchronization. Periodically, nodes compare their state with peers to detect and resolve any inconsistencies that weren't caught by regular synchronization mechanisms. This provides a safety net for ensuring eventual consistency across the cluster.

• • • •

MONITORING AND DEBUGGING distributed state becomes crucial at scale. We implement comprehensive logging and metrics collection for state synchronization events. This includes tracking synchronization latency, conflict rates, and state divergence between nodes. These metrics help us identify and diagnose synchronization issues before they impact users.

• • • •

NETWORK PARTITION HANDLING requires explicit consideration. When network issues prevent nodes from communicating, we need strategies for handling divergent state. We implement a system that tracks network partition events and initiates state reconciliation when connectivity is restored. This includes resolving any conflicts that occurred during the partition.

• • • •

FINALLY, WE CONSIDER deployment implications for state synchronization. Rolling deployments can temporarily result in different versions of code handling the same state. We implement backward and forward compatibility in our state synchronization protocols, ensuring that nodes running different versions can still communicate effectively during deployments.

• • • •

THROUGH THESE IMPLEMENTATIONS, we create a robust system for maintaining synchronized state across a distributed Phoenix application. While perfect consistency is impossible in distributed systems, our careful attention to state synchronization ensures that our application remains reliable and consistent enough for practical use cases.

# 28. Building a Distributed Chat System

Building a distributed chat system brings together many of the concepts we've covered throughout this book. A robust chat system must handle thousands of concurrent connections, maintain consistent state across multiple server nodes, and provide real-time message delivery while remaining scalable and fault-tolerant. In this chapter, we'll build a distributed chat system that demonstrates these principles in action.

• • • •

OUR DISTRIBUTED CHAT architecture builds on Phoenix's strengths in handling WebSocket connections and real-time communication. Each chat server node runs independently, capable of handling client connections and message processing. These nodes communicate through Phoenix PubSub, forming a mesh network where messages can flow efficiently between any connected clients, regardless of which node they're connected to.

• • • •

MESSAGE ROUTING FORMS the core of our distributed chat system. When a client sends a message, it first arrives at their connected node. This node becomes responsible for several critical tasks: persisting the message to the database, broadcasting it to other nodes via PubSub, and handling any necessary side effects like notifications or webhooks. This distribution of responsibility ensures that message processing continues even if some nodes fail.

• • • •

STATE MANAGEMENT IN our distributed chat system requires careful consideration. While message delivery is our primary concern, we also need to track user presence, maintain room memberships, and handle typing indicators. We use Phoenix Presence for user state, leveraging its CRDT properties to maintain consistent presence information across nodes. Room state is maintained through a combination of database records and in-memory caches, with careful synchronization between nodes.

• • • •

HERE'S HOW MESSAGE flow works in our system: When a client sends a message, their connected node first validates and processes it. The node then pushes the message to a persistent message queue, ensuring reliable delivery even during system disruptions. Other nodes subscribe to relevant message queues based on their connected clients' room memberships. This queue-based approach provides a buffer against network issues and helps handle back-pressure during high-load situations.

• • • •

PERFORMANCE OPTIMIZATION becomes crucial at scale. We implement several strategies to maintain responsive performance even with thousands of concurrent users. Message batching combines multiple messages into single broadcasts when appropriate. Connection pooling manages database connections efficiently across nodes. Smart partitioning ensures that frequently interacting users tend to connect to the same nodes, reducing inter-node communication.

• • • •

ERROR HANDLING AND recovery are critical in a distributed system. Each node implements comprehensive error handling for various failure scenarios: network partitions, database connectivity issues, or process crashes. When a node detects a failure, it attempts to recover gracefully while maintaining service for its connected clients. If recovery isn't possible, the node coordinates with others to redistribute its clients.

• • • •

MESSAGE PERSISTENCE requires careful database design. We implement a sharded database approach where messages are partitioned across multiple database instances based on chat room ID. This allows for efficient scaling of storage and prevents any single database from becoming a bottleneck. Each message record includes metadata like timestamps, read receipts, and delivery status, enabling features like message history and unread counts.

• • • •

REAL-TIME FEATURES extend beyond basic message delivery. Our system implements typing indicators through presence metadata, showing when users are composing messages. Read receipts track message delivery and viewing status across nodes. User status updates (online, away, offline) are distributed through presence channels, ensuring all clients have current information about other users' availability.

• • • •

SECURITY REMAINS PARAMOUNT in our distributed chat system. We implement end-to-end message encryption for private chats, ensuring messages can't be read by intermediate nodes. Authentication tokens are validated at each node independently, allowing for efficient connection handling without central authentication servers. Rate limiting is implemented both per-connection and per-node to prevent abuse.

• • • •

MONITORING AND OBSERVABILITY become crucial for operating a distributed chat system. We implement comprehensive metrics collection across all nodes, tracking message delivery latency, node health, connection counts, and error rates. These metrics feed into alerting systems that can notify operators of potential issues before they impact users.

• • • •

ADMINISTRATIVE FEATURES help manage the system at scale. We implement tools for moderating chat rooms, managing user access, and monitoring system health. These admin functions work across all nodes, allowing operators to manage the entire system from any entry point. Audit logging tracks administrative actions for accountability and troubleshooting.

• • • •

SCALING STRATEGIES focus on horizontal growth. When traffic increases, we can add more nodes to the cluster dynamically. New nodes automatically join the PubSub network and begin sharing the connection load. Database sharding allows for parallel scaling of persistence layers. Load balancers distribute incoming connections across available nodes while maintaining WebSocket connection stability.

• • • •

FAULT TOLERANCE IS built into every layer of the system. If a node fails, its clients can reconnect to other nodes without losing messages. Message queues ensure reliable delivery even during node transitions. Database replication provides redundancy for persistent data. The system continues operating even with multiple node failures, though perhaps with reduced capacity.

• • • •

DEPLOYMENT CONSIDERATIONS include strategies for zero-downtime updates. We implement rolling deployments where nodes are updated one at a time, allowing the system to continue operating during upgrades. Version compatibility between nodes ensures that different versions can coexist during deployment transitions. Database migrations are carefully coordinated to maintain backward compatibility.

• • • •

THROUGH THESE IMPLEMENTATIONS, we create a robust distributed chat system that demonstrates the power of Phoenix for real-time applications. The system handles scale through careful architecture, maintains consistency through distributed state management, and provides reliability through comprehensive error handling and recovery mechanisms.

# 29. Handling Network Partitions

Network partitions represent one of the most challenging aspects of distributed systems, and handling them gracefully is crucial for maintaining system reliability. In distributed Elixir applications, network partitions occur when nodes in a cluster become unable to communicate with each other, effectively splitting the cluster into isolated segments. This chapter explores strategies for detecting, managing, and recovering from network partitions in real time Phoenix applications.

The first line of defense against network partitions is early detection. Erlang's built-in distribution protocol automatically monitors node connections and can detect when nodes become unreachable. However, we need to implement additional logic to handle these scenarios appropriately. A common approach is to use the :net_kernel.monitor_nodes/1 function to receive notifications when nodes join or leave the cluster:

In your application's supervision tree, you might implement a dedicated GenServer that monitors node connections and maintains the cluster state. This process can track which nodes are currently available and coordinate the system's response to partition events. When a node becomes unreachable, the monitor will receive a nodedown message, allowing you to take appropriate action.

One of the most critical considerations when handling network partitions is data consistency. In a distributed chat system, for example, messages sent during a partition might not reach all intended recipients. There are several strategies to handle this situation. The simplest approach is to accept eventual consistency, where messages are delivered to available nodes and synchronized later when the partition heals. This approach prioritizes availability over consistency, following the AP (Availability and Partition Tolerance) properties of the CAP theorem.

For applications requiring stronger consistency guarantees, you might implement a quorum-based approach. This ensures that operations only proceed when a majority of nodes can participate. For example, you might require that at least 51% of nodes acknowledge a message before considering it successfully delivered. While this provides stronger consistency guarantees, it comes at the cost of reduced availability during network partitions.

Another crucial aspect of partition handling is state recovery. When a partition heals and nodes reconnect, you need mechanisms to reconcile potentially divergent state. Conflict-free Replicated Data Types (CRDTs) can be particularly useful here, as they provide mathematical guarantees about state convergence. For example, you might use a G-Counter CRDT to track message counts across nodes, ensuring that counters eventually reach the same value regardless of network partitions.

Phoenix PubSub plays a crucial role in partition handling. When using distributed Phoenix.PubSub, messages published during a partition will only reach subscribers connected to nodes within the same partition. To handle this, you might implement a message buffer that stores messages during partition events:

The buffer can then be used to replay messages when the partition heals, ensuring that all nodes eventually receive all messages. However, care must be taken to handle message ordering and deduplication, as messages might arrive multiple times or in different orders on different nodes.

For applications handling sensitive operations, such as financial transactions, you might need to implement a more conservative approach. One strategy is to designate certain operations as partition-sensitive and restrict them during partition events. This can be implemented using a distributed lock mechanism:

When implementing this approach, it's essential to handle timeout scenarios appropriately. If a node cannot acquire a lock within a reasonable timeframe, it should assume a partition has occurred and take appropriate action, such as failing over to a backup system or entering a degraded operation mode.

Monitoring and logging become especially important during partition events. Your application should maintain detailed logs of partition detection, duration, and recovery events. This information is invaluable for post-mortem analysis and system optimization. Consider implementing metrics that track:

- Partition frequency and duration
- Message delivery success rates during partitions
- State divergence metrics
- Recovery time after partition healing
- Resource usage during recovery operations

Testing partition scenarios is crucial but challenging. Tools like toxiproxy can help simulate network partitions in development and testing environments. You should regularly test your application's behavior under various partition scenarios, including:

- Complete node isolation
- Partial network connectivity
- Intermittent connectivity
- Multiple simultaneous partitions
- Long-duration partitions

Recovery procedures should be automated wherever possible. When a partition heals, your system should automatically:

- Detect the reconnection event
- Verify the health of reconnected nodes
- Initiate state synchronization
- Resume normal operations
- Log recovery metrics

It's also important to consider the human factor in partition handling. Your application should provide clear indicators of partition status to operators and users. This might include:

- Administrative dashboards showing cluster health
- User notifications about degraded service
- Automatic incident reports
- Recovery progress indicators

Performance considerations are crucial when implementing partition handling mechanisms. State synchronization after a partition heals can be resource-intensive, potentially impacting system performance. Consider implementing:

- Incremental state synchronization
- Background recovery processes
- Rate limiting for recovery operations
- Priority queues for critical state updates

Finally, remember that network partitions are often symptoms of underlying infrastructure issues. While robust partition handling is essential, you should also invest in:

- Network redundancy
- Infrastructure monitoring
- Automatic failover mechanisms
- Regular disaster recovery testing

By implementing these strategies and maintaining a comprehensive approach to partition handling, your distributed Phoenix application can maintain reliability and consistency even in the face of network disruptions. Remember that the specific approach you choose should be guided by your application's requirements regarding consistency, availability, and partition tolerance.

# 30. Load Balancing WebSocket Connections

Load balancing WebSocket connections is a critical aspect of scaling real time Phoenix applications to handle large numbers of concurrent users. Unlike traditional HTTP requests, WebSocket connections are long lived and maintain persistent state, which introduces unique challenges for load distribution and system scalability.

The most fundamental consideration when load balancing WebSocket connections is connection stickiness. Once a WebSocket connection is established with a particular server node, it needs to maintain that connection for its entire lifecycle. This requires configuring load balancers to support sticky sessions, ensuring that all subsequent communications from a client are routed to the same server that holds their WebSocket connection.

There are several approaches to implementing sticky sessions with WebSocket connections. One common method is to use cookie based session affinity, where the load balancer assigns a cookie to the client during the initial HTTP upgrade request to WebSocket. This cookie is then used to route all subsequent communications to the appropriate server. For example, when using HAProxy, you might configure session stickiness like this:

Another approach is to use IP based affinity, where the load balancer routes connections based on the client's IP address. This method can be simpler to implement but may not distribute load as evenly, especially when multiple clients share the same IP address through NAT.

Connection distribution strategies play a crucial role in maintaining balanced server load. The simplest approach is round robin distribution, where new connections are assigned to servers in sequence. However, this may not be optimal for WebSocket applications where connections have varying resource requirements. More sophisticated strategies might consider factors like:

Server load metrics including CPU usage, memory consumption, and current connection count

Geographic proximity to clients to minimize latency

Connection type and expected resource usage based on client behavior patterns

Monitoring becomes especially important when load balancing WebSocket connections. Your monitoring system should track metrics specific to WebSocket behavior, such as connection duration, message frequency, and payload sizes. This data can inform automatic scaling decisions and help identify potential bottlenecks.

Health checks require special consideration for WebSocket servers. Traditional HTTP health checks may not accurately reflect a server's ability to handle additional WebSocket connections. Consider implementing dedicated health check endpoints that report WebSocket specific metrics, such as current connection count, message processing rates, and available capacity.

One challenging aspect of load balancing WebSocket connections is handling server failures or maintenance events. When a server needs to be removed from the pool, its existing WebSocket connections need to be handled gracefully. There are several strategies for this:

Connection draining, where the server is marked as unavailable for new connections but continues serving existing ones until they naturally terminate

Forced disconnection with reconnection logic, where clients are programmed to automatically reconnect, potentially to a different server

State transfer, where connection state is migrated to another server before termination

Scaling operations also require careful handling. When adding new servers to the pool, you'll want to ensure that connections are distributed gradually to avoid overwhelming the new instances. Similarly, when scaling down, you'll need to carefully manage the migration of existing connections.

The choice of load balancer technology can significantly impact your system's performance and capabilities. Popular options include:

HAProxy, which offers excellent performance and detailed configuration options

NGINX Plus, which provides commercial features specifically for WebSocket handling

Cloud provider load balancers, which often integrate well with auto scaling capabilities

Each option has its own strengths and considerations. HAProxy, for example, excels at low level TCP handling and offers detailed monitoring capabilities. NGINX Plus provides advanced features like session persistence and active health checks. Cloud provider solutions often offer the simplest integration with existing infrastructure but may have limitations in terms of customization.

Rate limiting at the load balancer level becomes important as your system scales. While application level rate limiting is still necessary, implementing basic rate limiting at the load balancer can help protect your system from denial of service attacks and excessive connection attempts. Consider implementing limits on:

New connection rates per IP address

Message rates per connection

Concurrent connection counts per client

Connection pooling can help manage large numbers of WebSocket connections efficiently. By maintaining a pool of server side resources and reusing them across connections, you can reduce the overhead associated with connection establishment and management.

Geographic distribution of servers introduces additional complexity to load balancing. When operating across multiple regions, you might implement a hierarchical load balancing strategy:

Global load balancers direct clients to the nearest regional deployment

Regional load balancers distribute connections among local servers

Cross region communication handles cases where users need to interact across regions

Fault tolerance should be built into your load balancing strategy. This might include:

Multiple load balancer instances for redundancy

Automatic failover mechanisms

Regular backup and recovery testing

Monitoring and alerting for load balancer health

Security considerations at the load balancer level are crucial. Your load balancing infrastructure should implement:

TLS termination and certificate management

DDoS protection mechanisms

Access control lists and IP filtering

Protocol validation and sanitization

Performance optimization at the load balancer level can significantly impact your system's overall efficiency. Consider techniques such as:

TCP connection pooling

Buffer size optimization

Compression settings for WebSocket frames

Timeout configurations

Documentation and operational procedures become increasingly important as your load balancing infrastructure grows. Maintain detailed documentation covering:

Load balancer configuration parameters

Scaling procedures

Troubleshooting guides

Emergency response procedures

Finally, remember that load balancing is just one part of a comprehensive scaling strategy. It should work in concert with other system components like database scaling, caching layers, and application level optimizations to provide a robust and scalable real time system.

# 31. Database Optimization for Real-Time Apps

Database optimization plays a crucial role in building performant real time applications with Phoenix and Elixir. While WebSocket connections and LiveView handle the real time aspects of our applications, the database often becomes the bottleneck when scaling to handle large numbers of concurrent users and real time updates.

The first consideration in optimizing databases for real time applications is understanding the access patterns specific to real time features. Unlike traditional web applications where database interactions are primarily triggered by HTTP requests, real time applications often require continuous database operations to keep connected clients in sync. This might include polling for updates, handling real time inserts and updates, and managing presence information.

One of the most important optimizations is proper indexing for real time queries. Consider a chat application where messages need to be retrieved in real time. Without proper indexes, each query might require a full table scan, leading to poor performance as the dataset grows. Indexes should be carefully chosen based on query patterns, but be cautious of over indexing, which can slow down write operations. Partial indexes can be particularly useful for real time applications, allowing you to index only the most recent or relevant data.

Connection pooling becomes especially important in real time applications. Ecto, the database library commonly used with Phoenix, provides connection pooling out of the box, but the pool size needs to be carefully tuned based on your application's needs. Too few connections can lead to bottlenecks, while too many can overwhelm the database server. Consider that each Phoenix channel or LiveView process might need database access, and size your connection pool accordingly.

Read/write splitting can significantly improve performance for real time applications with heavy read loads. By directing read queries to replica databases, you can reduce the load on your primary database and improve response times for real time updates. However, this introduces eventual consistency considerations that need to be carefully managed in your application logic.

Query optimization takes on new importance in real time contexts. Long running queries can block other operations and impact real time responsiveness. Use database explain plans to understand query performance and optimize accordingly. Consider breaking down complex queries into smaller operations that can be executed asynchronously. Be particularly careful with N+1 query problems, which can be especially problematic in real time applications where data is frequently refreshed.

Database partitioning strategies can help manage large datasets in real time applications. Time based partitioning is often effective for real time data, allowing you to efficiently query recent data while maintaining historical records. For example, in a real time analytics application, you might partition data by day or hour to optimize queries for current activity.

Batch operations become crucial for handling high volume real time updates. Instead of updating records individually, consider batching updates together. Ecto.Multi provides an excellent way to handle multiple database operations as a single transaction. This can be particularly effective when combined with GenServer processes that buffer and batch updates.

Caching strategies at the database level can significantly improve performance. Consider using materialized views for complex aggregate queries that are frequently accessed in real time. Database level caching differs from application level caching in that it maintains consistency with the underlying data automatically.

Change data capture (CDC) patterns can be valuable for real time applications. Instead of polling for changes, you can use database features like PostgreSQL's LISTEN/NOTIFY to receive real time notifications of data changes. This can be more efficient than polling and provides lower latency for real time updates.

Query timeouts need careful consideration in real time contexts. Long running queries can block database connections and impact real time responsiveness. Set appropriate timeout values and implement retry logic where necessary. Consider using timeout options at both the database and application levels.

Monitoring database performance becomes even more critical in real time applications. Track key metrics like query execution time, connection pool utilization, and lock contention. Set up alerts for anomalies that could impact real time performance. Tools like pg_stat_statements can provide valuable insights into query performance patterns.

Database cleanup strategies need to account for real time operation. Regular maintenance operations like vacuum and index rebuilding need to be scheduled carefully to minimize impact on real time functionality. Consider implementing data retention policies that automatically archive or delete old data to maintain performance.

Error handling at the database level requires special attention in real time applications. Network issues, deadlocks, or other database problems need to be handled gracefully to maintain real time functionality. Implement appropriate retry logic and fallback mechanisms to handle temporary database unavailability.

Schema design plays a crucial role in database performance for real time applications. Consider denormalization where appropriate to optimize for read performance. Use appropriate data types and constraints to maintain data integrity while minimizing overhead. Be particularly careful with table relationships that might impact real time query performance.

Finally, remember that database optimization is an ongoing process. Regular monitoring and tuning based on actual usage patterns is essential. Keep track of how database performance metrics change as your application scales and be prepared to adjust your optimization strategies accordingly.

The key to successful database optimization for real time applications is finding the right balance between consistency, performance, and complexity. Each optimization technique comes with its own tradeoffs that need to be evaluated in the context of your specific application requirements.

# 32. Caching Strategies

Caching plays a vital role in improving the performance and scalability of real time Phoenix applications. When implemented correctly, caching can significantly reduce database load, improve response times, and help handle traffic spikes more effectively.

In real time applications, caching strategies need to be carefully designed to balance data freshness with performance. Unlike traditional web applications where data might be relatively static, real time applications often deal with frequently changing data that needs to be propagated to connected clients quickly.

ETS (Erlang Term Storage) tables provide an excellent in memory caching solution for Phoenix applications. ETS tables store data in memory and provide concurrent access with different read/write patterns. For real time applications, consider using ETS tables to cache frequently accessed data that needs to be shared across multiple processes. ETS tables are particularly useful for caching presence information, connection states, or lookup data that changes infrequently.

Distributed caching becomes important when running Phoenix applications across multiple nodes. Erlang's built in distributed features can be leveraged to create a distributed cache using :global or :pg2 modules. However, for more complex caching needs, consider using dedicated caching solutions like Redis or Memcached. These systems provide additional features like automatic key expiration, atomic operations, and pub/sub capabilities that can be valuable for real time applications.

Cache invalidation strategies are crucial for maintaining data consistency. In real time applications, stale cache data can lead to confusing user experiences. Consider implementing cache invalidation patterns like write through (update cache and database simultaneously) or write behind (update cache immediately and database asynchronously). The choice depends on your specific consistency requirements and performance needs.

Application level caching can be implemented using Phoenix's built in caching mechanisms. The Phoenix.View.render_many function, for example, can cache rendered templates. For LiveView applications, consider caching expensive computations or database queries that don't need to be refreshed on every client update.

Fragment caching can be particularly effective for real time applications that combine dynamic and static content. By caching portions of your LiveView templates that change infrequently, you can reduce the processing overhead while still maintaining real time updates for dynamic content.

Cache warming strategies should be considered for data that needs to be immediately available. When starting your Phoenix application or adding new nodes to a cluster, implement cache warming procedures to populate frequently accessed data. This prevents a flood of database queries when the application first starts handling traffic.

Memory management becomes crucial when implementing caching strategies. Monitor cache size and implement eviction policies to prevent memory issues. Consider using tools like :observer to monitor memory usage across your application, including cache storage.

Cache consistency across nodes requires careful consideration in distributed systems. Implement mechanisms to propagate cache invalidation messages across all nodes in your cluster. Phoenix PubSub can be used effectively for this purpose, allowing nodes to coordinate cache updates and invalidations.

Query caching patterns can significantly improve performance for complex or expensive queries. Consider caching query results with appropriate time to live (TTL) values based on how frequently the underlying data changes. Implement cache stampede prevention using techniques like the dogpile effect lock.

Real time specific caching patterns might include caching WebSocket connection details, user session information, or temporary state that needs to be quickly accessible across different processes. Consider using process registry patterns with ETS tables to maintain this type of ephemeral cache data.

Caching layers should be designed with failure scenarios in mind. Implement fallback mechanisms for when cache servers become unavailable. Consider using circuit breaker patterns to prevent cascade failures when cache systems experience issues.

Cache monitoring and metrics are essential for maintaining performance. Track cache hit rates, miss rates, and invalidation patterns. Set up alerts for unusual patterns that might indicate cache related issues. Tools like Telemetry can be used to collect and analyze cache performance metrics.

Version based caching can be effective for handling real time updates. Instead of invalidating cache entries directly, maintain version numbers for cached resources and increment them when updates occur. This can help prevent race conditions in distributed environments.

Consider implementing multi level caching strategies for different types of data. Frequently accessed, rarely changed data might be cached indefinitely in ETS tables, while more dynamic data might use shorter lived Redis caches. This tiered approach can help optimize both performance and resource usage.

Periodic cache maintenance should be implemented to prevent memory leaks and ensure optimal performance. Schedule regular cleanup of expired cache entries and monitor cache size growth over time. Implement automated processes to detect and remove orphaned cache entries.

The choice of caching strategy should be driven by your application's specific requirements and constraints. Consider factors like data consistency needs, update frequency, read/write patterns, and scaling requirements when designing your caching architecture.

Testing caching implementations thoroughly is crucial. Write tests that verify cache invalidation behavior, consistency across nodes, and proper handling of race conditions. Consider using property based testing to uncover edge cases in cache behavior.

Finally, remember that caching is not a silver bullet for performance issues. Each caching decision should be based on measured performance improvements and careful consideration of the maintenance overhead introduced. Regular monitoring and adjustment of caching strategies is essential for maintaining optimal performance as your application evolves.

## 33. Message Queue Integration

Message Queue Integration plays a crucial role in building scalable real time Phoenix applications, particularly when dealing with high throughput and distributed systems. Message queues provide a reliable way to handle asynchronous processing, decouple system components, and ensure reliable message delivery in distributed environments.

RabbitMQ is often the message queue of choice for Phoenix applications due to its excellent Erlang implementation and natural fit within the BEAM ecosystem. Setting up RabbitMQ integration begins with adding the appropriate dependencies to your Phoenix application. The amqp package provides a solid foundation for interacting with RabbitMQ, while the broadway package offers powerful abstractions for building data processing pipelines.

When integrating message queues with Phoenix applications, it's important to consider the various message patterns available. The publish/subscribe pattern works well for broadcasting messages to multiple consumers, making it ideal for real time updates that need to be propagated to multiple clients. The work queue pattern, on the other hand, is perfect for distributing time consuming tasks across multiple workers.

Message durability becomes a critical consideration when implementing queue based systems. Durable queues ensure messages persist even if the broker restarts, while transient queues might be more appropriate for ephemeral data that can be safely lost in case of failure. The choice between these options depends on your application's specific reliability requirements.

Error handling in message queue systems requires careful consideration. Implement dead letter queues to capture messages that fail processing, allowing for later analysis or retry attempts. Consider implementing retry mechanisms with exponential backoff for temporary failures, while permanent failures should be logged and possibly alerted on.

Queue monitoring becomes essential as your system scales. Implement monitoring for queue depths, processing rates, and error rates. Tools like Prometheus and Grafana can be used to visualize queue metrics and set up alerting for abnormal conditions. Consider implementing circuit breakers to prevent queue overflow during high load situations.

Message serialization formats need to be chosen carefully. While JSON is common, consider using more efficient formats like Protocol Buffers or MessagePack for high throughput scenarios. Ensure your serialization strategy includes version handling to support future message format changes without breaking existing consumers.

Consumer concurrency needs to be managed effectively. Phoenix applications can leverage the BEAM's concurrency model to process messages in parallel. Use supervised GenServer processes to manage queue consumers, and consider implementing consumer pools to handle varying loads efficiently.

Message routing strategies become important as your application grows. Consider implementing routing based on message content, allowing different types of messages to be processed by specialized consumers. This can help with scaling specific parts of your system independently based on load patterns.

Back pressure mechanisms should be implemented to prevent system overload. Use queue size limits and consumer rate limiting to ensure your system degrades gracefully under heavy load. Consider implementing flow control mechanisms between producers and consumers to maintain system stability.

Integration testing of queue based systems requires careful consideration. Set up test environments with isolated queue instances, and implement helpers for testing queue based functionality. Consider using test doubles for queue interactions during unit testing to improve test speed and reliability.

Queue based architectures often benefit from implementing the Command Query Responsibility Segregation (CQRS) pattern. Use message queues to handle command processing asynchronously while maintaining separate optimized read models for queries. This can significantly improve system scalability and responsiveness.

Message queue clustering becomes important for high availability setups. Configure queue clusters to ensure message processing continues even if individual nodes fail. Implement appropriate monitoring and failover procedures for your queue infrastructure.

Performance optimization of queue based systems involves several aspects. Consider batch processing messages when appropriate, optimize message payload sizes, and implement appropriate prefetch settings for consumers. Monitor and tune these settings based on your specific workload patterns.

Security considerations for message queues include authentication, authorization, and encryption. Implement appropriate access controls for queue operations, and consider encrypting sensitive message content. Use SSL/TLS for queue connections in production environments.

Queue management tools can significantly improve operational efficiency. Consider implementing administrative interfaces for monitoring queue status, managing dead letter queues, and performing maintenance tasks. Tools like RabbitMQ Management Plugin provide valuable insights into queue operation.

Error recovery procedures should be well defined for queue based systems. Implement procedures for handling queue server failures, message processing failures, and network issues. Consider implementing automatic failover and recovery procedures where appropriate.

Message queue patterns can be effectively combined with Phoenix PubSub for real time updates. Use queues for reliable message processing and PubSub for real time client notifications. This combination provides both reliability and real time responsiveness.

Queue based architectures should be designed with scalability in mind. Consider implementing message partitioning strategies to allow horizontal scaling of consumers. Design message flows to minimize dependencies between different parts of your system.

Finally, remember that message queues add complexity to your system. Carefully evaluate whether the benefits of queue based processing outweigh the additional operational complexity for your specific use case. Start with simpler patterns and evolve your queue architecture based on actual needs and performance requirements.

# 34. Building an IoT Monitoring System

Building an IoT monitoring system with Phoenix presents unique challenges and opportunities for leveraging real time capabilities. IoT devices generate continuous streams of data that need to be collected, processed, and analyzed in real time to provide meaningful insights and enable timely actions.

The foundation of an IoT monitoring system starts with establishing reliable WebSocket connections for device communication. Phoenix Channels provide an excellent mechanism for handling these connections, allowing bidirectional communication between IoT devices and the server. Each device can connect to a dedicated channel, enabling individual device monitoring and control.

Data ingestion requires careful consideration of message formats and protocols. While MQTT is a popular protocol for IoT communications, WebSocket based communication through Phoenix Channels can provide similar functionality with the added benefit of seamless integration with your Phoenix application. Structure your messages to include essential metadata such as device identifiers, timestamps, and message types.

Device state management becomes crucial when dealing with numerous connected devices. Implement a state management system using GenServers to track device status, connection health, and latest readings. This state can be used to detect offline devices, track device history, and manage device configurations.

Real time data processing pipelines are essential for handling the continuous stream of device data. Implement processing stages for data validation, transformation, and aggregation. Consider using Broadway for building robust data processing pipelines that can handle high throughput scenarios while providing back pressure mechanisms.

Time series data storage requires special consideration. Traditional relational databases might not be optimal for storing high frequency sensor data. Consider using specialized time series databases like TimescaleDB or InfluxDB for efficient storage and querying of sensor data. Implement data retention policies to manage storage growth.

Alerting mechanisms form a critical component of IoT monitoring systems. Implement threshold based alerts using GenServers to monitor device readings and trigger notifications when values exceed defined thresholds. Consider implementing different alert severity levels and notification channels like email, SMS, or push notifications.

Device provisioning and management functionality should be built into the system. Implement secure device registration processes, manage device credentials, and provide interfaces for updating device configurations. Consider implementing device groups or zones for easier management of large device fleets.

Data visualization becomes essential for making sense of IoT data. Phoenix LiveView excels at building real time dashboards that can display current device status, historical trends, and alert conditions. Implement interactive visualizations that allow users to explore data and customize their view of device information.

System scalability needs careful consideration when dealing with potentially thousands of connected devices. Implement connection pooling, load balancing, and proper supervision trees to handle device connections efficiently. Consider sharding device connections across multiple nodes in a distributed setup.

Device authentication and authorization require robust security measures. Implement device specific credentials, possibly using client certificates for enhanced security. Consider implementing rate limiting per device to prevent individual devices from overwhelming the system.

Data buffering and retry mechanisms are essential for handling network interruptions. Implement local buffering on devices when possible, and design server side systems to handle reconnections and data backfill scenarios gracefully. Consider implementing store and forward patterns for critical data.

Analytics capabilities can provide valuable insights from device data. Implement both real time analytics for immediate insights and batch processing for deeper historical analysis. Consider implementing machine learning models for anomaly detection or predictive maintenance.

Edge computing patterns can be valuable for reducing server load and network traffic. Consider implementing data preprocessing and aggregation at the edge, possibly using Nerves for running Elixir on edge devices. This can help reduce bandwidth usage and provide faster local response times.

System monitoring becomes crucial at scale. Implement comprehensive monitoring of device connections, data processing pipelines, and system resources. Set up alerting for system level issues that could affect device communication or data processing.

Data archival strategies need to account for long term storage requirements. Implement data aggregation and archival processes to maintain historical data while managing storage costs. Consider implementing data export capabilities for external analysis or backup purposes.

Integration with external systems might be necessary for comprehensive monitoring. Implement APIs for external system integration, and consider implementing standard protocols like REST or GraphQL for data access. Design these integrations with security and scalability in mind.

Firmware update capabilities might be required for connected devices. Implement secure firmware update mechanisms, possibly using Phoenix Channels for firmware distribution. Consider implementing staged rollouts and rollback capabilities for firmware updates.

Testing IoT systems requires comprehensive approaches. Implement device simulators for testing at scale, and consider implementing chaos engineering practices to verify system resilience. Develop automated tests for device communication, data processing, and alerting functionality.

Documentation becomes crucial for system maintenance and troubleshooting. Maintain comprehensive documentation of device protocols, data formats, and system architecture. Consider implementing system wide logging with correlation IDs to track device interactions through the system.

The success of an IoT monitoring system often depends on finding the right balance between real time capabilities and system reliability. Focus on building robust foundations that can scale with your device fleet while maintaining responsive real time monitoring capabilities.

# 35. Handling Device Connections

Handling device connections in an IoT monitoring system requires careful consideration of connection management, scalability, and reliability. When dealing with thousands or potentially millions of connected devices, proper connection handling becomes crucial for system stability and performance.

Connection establishment should follow a well defined handshake protocol. Upon initial connection, devices should provide authentication credentials and basic metadata such as device type, firmware version, and capabilities. This information helps establish the device context and determines how the system will handle subsequent communications.

Connection persistence requires implementing proper heartbeat mechanisms. While WebSocket connections include built in ping/pong frames, additional application level heartbeats can provide better insight into device health. Consider implementing variable heartbeat intervals based on device type and network conditions to balance responsiveness with system load.

Connection pooling becomes essential when dealing with large numbers of devices. Implement connection pools using supervision trees to manage connection processes efficiently. Each pool can handle a subset of devices, allowing for better resource utilization and simplified management. Consider implementing dynamic pool sizing based on current system load and connection patterns.

Error handling for device connections must be robust and graceful. Implement proper error recovery mechanisms that can handle various failure scenarios, from network interruptions to device malfunctions. Consider implementing exponential backoff strategies for reconnection attempts to prevent connection storms during system recovery.

Connection state management requires careful tracking of device status. Implement a state machine for each connection that tracks the current connection phase, from initial handshake through active operation to graceful disconnection. This state information can be used to make intelligent decisions about connection handling and resource allocation.

Load balancing becomes crucial when handling connections across multiple nodes. Implement consistent hashing or similar strategies to distribute device connections across available nodes while maintaining connection affinity. Consider implementing connection migration capabilities for handling node failures or maintenance scenarios.

Connection monitoring needs to provide insights into system health. Implement metrics collection for connection statistics, including connection duration, failure rates, and latency measurements. These metrics can help identify potential issues before they become critical problems.

Rate limiting should be implemented at the connection level to prevent individual devices from overwhelming the system. Consider implementing token bucket algorithms or similar rate limiting strategies that can handle burst traffic while maintaining overall system stability. Implement different rate limit tiers based on device type or service level agreements.

Connection security requires ongoing validation beyond initial authentication. Implement periodic credential validation and consider implementing capability based authorization for different device operations. Monitor connection patterns for potential security issues such as unusual connection attempts or suspicious traffic patterns.

Buffer management becomes important when dealing with connection interruptions. Implement appropriate buffer sizes for incoming and outgoing messages, considering both memory usage and potential data loss scenarios. Consider implementing different buffering strategies based on message priority and system load.

Connection cleanup requires careful attention to resource management. Implement proper cleanup procedures for terminated connections, ensuring all associated resources are properly released. Consider implementing periodic cleanup tasks to handle any orphaned resources that might accumulate over time.

Scaling connection handling requires careful system design. Consider implementing connection sharding strategies that allow for horizontal scaling of connection handling capacity. Implement proper monitoring and alerting for connection related metrics to guide scaling decisions.

Connection metadata management helps maintain system organization. Implement efficient storage and retrieval mechanisms for connection related metadata, considering both immediate access needs and historical tracking requirements. Consider implementing tagging systems for easier connection management and troubleshooting.

Protocol versioning becomes important as systems evolve. Implement proper protocol version negotiation during connection establishment and consider maintaining backward compatibility for older device firmware versions. Implement graceful degradation capabilities for devices that don't support newer protocol features.

Connection prioritization might be necessary for handling resource constraints. Implement priority queues for connection handling and consider implementing quality of service levels for different device types or operations. Consider implementing fair queuing mechanisms to prevent starvation of lower priority connections.

Testing connection handling requires comprehensive approaches. Implement connection simulation capabilities that can test various failure scenarios and load conditions. Consider implementing chaos engineering practices specifically focused on connection handling to verify system resilience.

Documentation of connection handling becomes crucial for system maintenance. Maintain detailed documentation of connection protocols, state machines, and error handling procedures. Consider implementing detailed logging of connection related events for troubleshooting and audit purposes.

The success of device connection handling often depends on finding the right balance between system complexity and reliability. Focus on building robust, scalable connection handling mechanisms while maintaining system simplicity where possible. Regular review and optimization of connection handling strategies helps ensure continued system reliability as device fleets grow and evolve.

# 36. Real-Time Data Processing

Real-time data processing in IoT systems presents unique challenges and opportunities. The ability to process and analyze data streams from thousands of connected devices in real time requires careful architecture and implementation considerations. Let's explore the key aspects of building robust real-time data processing systems with Elixir and Phoenix.

At its core, real-time data processing requires efficient stream handling capabilities. Elixir's built-in Stream module provides powerful abstractions for working with potentially infinite data streams. When implementing stream processing for IoT data, consider breaking down the processing pipeline into distinct stages that can be supervised and scaled independently.

Data ingestion serves as the entry point for device telemetry. Implement buffer strategies that can handle sudden spikes in incoming data while maintaining system responsiveness. Consider using GenStage or Flow for back pressure handling, ensuring that downstream processing stages aren't overwhelmed during high load periods.

Data normalization becomes crucial when dealing with diverse device types. Implement transformation pipelines that can standardize data formats from different device versions or manufacturers. Consider implementing protocol adapters that can handle various input formats while maintaining consistent internal data structures.

Processing pipelines need to be both efficient and fault tolerant. Structure your processing stages using supervision trees, allowing individual stages to fail and recover without affecting the entire pipeline. Consider implementing circuit breakers for external service calls that might be part of your processing pipeline.

Real-time aggregation often requires maintaining running calculations across data streams. Implement efficient aggregation strategies using ETS tables or other in-memory storage solutions. Consider implementing sliding window calculations for time-based metrics while managing memory usage effectively.

Pattern detection becomes valuable for identifying important events in real time. Implement pattern matching algorithms that can detect significant changes or anomalies in data streams. Consider implementing different detection strategies based on device type and expected behavior patterns.

Data enrichment often requires combining real-time streams with historical or reference data. Implement caching strategies for frequently accessed reference data to minimize database load. Consider implementing predictive loading for related data based on observed patterns in the stream.

Processing prioritization becomes important when dealing with different types of data streams. Implement priority queues for critical data processing while ensuring fair handling of lower priority streams. Consider implementing adaptive prioritization based on current system load and business rules.

State management across processing stages requires careful consideration. Implement appropriate state storage mechanisms that balance access speed with durability requirements. Consider implementing state checkpointing for long-running calculations to enable recovery from failures.

Error handling in processing pipelines needs special attention. Implement appropriate error recovery mechanisms that can handle various failure scenarios without losing critical data. Consider implementing dead letter queues for messages that fail processing, allowing for later analysis and reprocessing.

Performance monitoring becomes crucial for real-time processing systems. Implement comprehensive metrics collection across all processing stages to identify bottlenecks and potential issues. Consider implementing adaptive processing strategies that can adjust based on current system performance.

Resource management requires careful attention to system capabilities. Implement appropriate resource allocation strategies that prevent any single processing stage from consuming excessive resources. Consider implementing load shedding mechanisms for handling extreme load conditions.

Data persistence strategies need to balance real-time processing needs with storage requirements. Implement efficient storage mechanisms that can handle high write loads while maintaining query performance. Consider implementing tiered storage strategies that move older data to lower cost storage options.

Processing optimization often requires ongoing tuning and adjustment. Implement performance profiling capabilities that can identify processing bottlenecks. Consider implementing A/B testing capabilities for comparing different processing strategies.

Scaling considerations become important as data volumes grow. Implement horizontal scaling capabilities for processing stages that can benefit from parallelization. Consider implementing dynamic scaling based on current processing load and latency requirements.

Integration with external systems often becomes necessary for comprehensive processing. Implement robust integration patterns that can handle external system failures gracefully. Consider implementing retry strategies with exponential backoff for external service calls.

Testing real-time processing systems requires specialized approaches. Implement comprehensive testing strategies that can verify processing accuracy under various load conditions. Consider implementing chaos engineering practices to verify system resilience.

The key to successful real-time data processing lies in finding the right balance between processing complexity and system reliability.

Focus on building robust, scalable processing pipelines while maintaining system maintainability. Regular review and optimization of processing strategies helps ensure continued system effectiveness as data volumes and processing requirements evolve.

# 37. Event Sourcing Patterns

Event sourcing represents a powerful architectural pattern for building real-time systems that need to maintain a complete history of state changes. In Phoenix applications, event sourcing can provide robust audit trails, enable complex analytics, and support system recovery. Let's explore how to effectively implement event sourcing patterns in real-time Phoenix applications.

Event sourcing fundamentally changes how we think about application state. Instead of storing the current state directly, we store a sequence of events that led to that state. Each event represents an immutable fact about something that happened in our system. This approach provides numerous benefits for real-time applications, particularly when dealing with complex domain models or when audit trails are essential.

In Phoenix applications, implementing event sourcing typically begins with defining your event schema. Events should be immutable and contain all necessary information to understand what happened at that moment. Consider using Ecto schemas to define your events, even if you're not storing them in a traditional relational database. This provides structure and validation while maintaining flexibility in storage options.

Stream processing becomes a natural fit when working with event sourced systems. Elixir's powerful stream abstractions make it straightforward to process event streams efficiently. Implement event handlers that can process streams of events to rebuild current state or calculate derived values. Consider using GenStage or Flow for handling high volume event streams with back pressure.

Event storage requires careful consideration. While any persistent storage can work, certain databases are particularly well suited for event sourcing. Consider using append only stores or specialized event stores that optimize for this use case. Implement storage strategies that can handle high write volumes while maintaining quick access to recent events.

Snapshots become important as event streams grow longer. Implement snapshot mechanisms that can periodically capture current state to optimize rebuilding. Consider implementing incremental snapshot strategies that can efficiently update existing snapshots with new events.

Projections allow you to derive different views of your data from the event stream. Implement projection handlers that can build and maintain these derived views in real time. Consider implementing caching strategies for frequently accessed projections to improve system performance.

Version management becomes crucial when working with long lived event streams. Implement event versioning strategies that can handle schema evolution over time. Consider implementing event upcasters that can transform older event versions to current schemas.

Command handling in event sourced systems requires special attention. Implement command handlers that validate business rules before generating events. Consider implementing command validation pipelines that can enforce complex business rules across multiple events.

Consistency boundaries need careful consideration in distributed systems. Implement appropriate consistency mechanisms that match your business requirements. Consider implementing event causality tracking to maintain logical consistency across distributed components.

Performance optimization often requires balancing between write and read performance. Implement caching strategies that can maintain frequently accessed projections in memory. Consider implementing batch processing for historical event replay while maintaining real-time processing for new events.

Error handling in event sourced systems presents unique challenges. Implement robust error handling that can maintain system consistency even during failures. Consider implementing compensation events that can correct errors in the event stream when necessary.

Testing event sourced systems requires comprehensive approaches. Implement testing strategies that can verify system behavior across complex event sequences. Consider implementing property based testing to verify system invariants across different event combinations.

Event sourcing particularly shines in scenarios requiring audit trails or complex analytics. Implement query capabilities that can analyze event streams for patterns or anomalies. Consider implementing event analytics that can provide insights into system behavior over time.

Integration with external systems requires careful handling of events across system boundaries. Implement integration strategies that can maintain consistency across system boundaries. Consider implementing event translation layers that can map between different event schemas.

Scaling event sourced systems often involves distributing event processing. Implement partitioning strategies that can distribute event processing across multiple nodes. Consider implementing event routing mechanisms that can maintain ordering guarantees where necessary.

The success of event sourcing implementations often depends on finding the right balance between complexity and benefit. Focus on areas where the additional complexity provides clear value, such as audit requirements or complex domain rules. Regular review of event schemas and processing patterns helps maintain system maintainability as requirements evolve.

Recovery capabilities become a key strength of event sourced systems. Implement recovery mechanisms that can rebuild system state from the event stream. Consider implementing parallel processing for faster recovery while maintaining event ordering guarantees.

Remember that event sourcing isn't always the right choice for every part of your system. Carefully evaluate where event sourcing provides clear benefits and consider hybrid approaches that use event sourcing alongside traditional state management where appropriate. The goal is to leverage event sourcing's strengths while maintaining system simplicity and maintainability.

# 38. CQRS in Phoenix Applications

CQRS (Command Query Responsibility Segregation) represents a powerful architectural pattern that naturally complements real time Phoenix applications. When implemented thoughtfully, CQRS allows systems to scale reads and writes independently while maintaining consistency and performance. Let's explore how to effectively implement CQRS in Phoenix applications.

At its core, CQRS separates an application's command operations (writes) from its query operations (reads). This separation allows each side to be optimized independently. In Phoenix applications, this often means maintaining separate data models and potentially separate databases for reads and writes. The command side handles all state changes while the query side focuses on providing optimized views of the data.

Implementing CQRS in Phoenix starts with clearly defining your command and query models. Command models focus on maintaining consistency and enforcing business rules. They typically use Ecto schemas that closely match your domain model. Query models, on the other hand, are optimized for specific read patterns and might denormalize data to improve query performance.

Phoenix Channels provide an excellent mechanism for handling commands in real time applications. Implement command handlers as Channel callbacks that validate input and process state changes. Consider implementing command validation pipelines that can enforce complex business rules before state changes are committed. Command handlers should focus on maintaining consistency while deferring any heavy computation or side effects.

The query side of CQRS systems often benefits from specialized data stores optimized for specific query patterns. Consider using separate databases or data structures that match your query requirements. Elasticsearch might be appropriate for full text search queries, while a graph database might better serve relationship based queries. The key is choosing data stores that naturally fit your query patterns.

Synchronization between command and query models requires careful consideration. Implement update mechanisms that can efficiently propagate changes from command models to query models. Consider using Phoenix PubSub to broadcast state changes to query model updaters. Implement eventual consistency patterns that can handle temporary inconsistencies between command and query models.

LiveView works particularly well with CQRS architectures. Implement LiveView modules that subscribe to relevant state changes and update their query models accordingly. Consider implementing view models specifically optimized for LiveView rendering. These view models can maintain denormalized data structures that minimize computation during render cycles.

Performance optimization in CQRS systems often focuses on managing the trade offs between consistency and availability. Implement caching strategies that can maintain frequently accessed query models in memory. Consider implementing background job processors that can handle heavy computation without impacting real time operations.

Error handling becomes more complex in CQRS systems due to the separation of concerns. Implement robust error handling that can maintain consistency between command and query models even during failures. Consider implementing compensation mechanisms that can correct inconsistencies when they occur.

Testing CQRS implementations requires comprehensive approaches that cover both command and query sides. Implement testing strategies that verify system behavior across complex state changes. Consider implementing integration tests that verify consistency between command and query models.

Scaling CQRS systems often involves distributing command and query processing across different nodes. Implement partitioning strategies that can distribute processing load while maintaining consistency. Consider implementing read replicas that can handle query load without impacting command processing.

The success of CQRS implementations often depends on finding the right granularity for command and query separation. Not every part of your system needs this separation. Focus on areas where the additional complexity provides clear benefits in terms of scalability or performance.

Command validation becomes particularly important in CQRS systems. Implement validation pipelines that can enforce business rules before state changes occur. Consider implementing domain events that can trigger side effects after successful command processing.

Query optimization often requires careful consideration of data access patterns. Implement query models that match your application's specific read requirements. Consider implementing materialized views that can cache complex query results while maintaining acceptable freshness.

Monitoring becomes crucial in CQRS systems due to their distributed nature. Implement monitoring strategies that can track consistency between command and query models. Consider implementing health checks that can verify system integrity across both sides.

Recovery capabilities need special attention in CQRS systems. Implement recovery mechanisms that can rebuild query models from command history when necessary. Consider implementing incremental update mechanisms that can efficiently synchronize query models with command state.

Remember that CQRS isn't always the right choice for every application. The pattern introduces complexity that needs to be justified by clear benefits in terms of scalability, performance, or maintenance. Carefully evaluate where CQRS provides value and consider simpler alternatives where appropriate.

# 39. Testing WebSocket Connections

Testing WebSocket connections represents a critical aspect of building reliable real time applications. A comprehensive testing strategy helps ensure your WebSocket implementation remains robust and reliable across different scenarios and edge cases. Let's explore effective approaches to testing WebSocket connections in Phoenix applications.

Testing WebSocket connections begins with understanding the various layers involved. At the lowest level, you need to verify the connection establishment process, including proper handshake negotiation and protocol upgrades. Phoenix provides testing utilities specifically designed for WebSocket testing through its Channel testing modules.

Socket authentication testing requires particular attention. Implement tests that verify proper token validation, connection parameter handling, and authentication failure scenarios. Consider testing various authentication methods, including token based authentication and custom authentication schemes. Your tests should verify that unauthorized connections are properly rejected and that authorized connections receive appropriate socket assignments.

Channel join operations represent another crucial testing area. Implement tests that verify proper topic subscription, initial state assignment, and join authorization. Your tests should cover both successful joins and various failure scenarios. Consider testing concurrent join operations to verify proper handling of race conditions.

Message handling tests should verify proper message routing and processing. Implement tests that verify message format validation, payload processing, and response generation. Consider testing various message types and formats to ensure robust handling of different communication patterns. Your tests should verify both successful message processing and proper error handling for invalid messages.

Connection lifecycle testing helps ensure proper handling of connection states. Implement tests that verify proper handling of connection establishment, maintenance, and termination. Consider testing various disconnect scenarios, including clean disconnects and unexpected connection drops. Your tests should verify proper cleanup of resources and state when connections terminate.

Broadcasting tests verify proper message distribution across connected clients. Implement tests that verify broadcast targeting, message delivery, and proper handling of broadcast failures. Consider testing various broadcast patterns, including room broadcasts, direct messages, and presence related broadcasts. Your tests should verify that messages reach their intended recipients while maintaining proper security boundaries.

Presence testing requires special consideration. Implement tests that verify proper tracking of user presence, including joins, leaves, and presence state updates. Consider testing presence synchronization across multiple nodes and proper handling of network partitions. Your tests should verify that presence information remains consistent across different scenarios.

Load testing WebSocket connections helps verify system behavior under stress. Implement tests that can simulate multiple concurrent connections and verify system performance under load. Consider testing various traffic patterns, including burst traffic and sustained high connection counts. Your tests should verify that system performance remains acceptable under expected load conditions.

Error handling tests verify proper system behavior during failure scenarios. Implement tests that verify proper handling of various error conditions, including network errors, protocol violations, and application errors. Consider testing error recovery mechanisms and proper state restoration after errors occur. Your tests should verify that the system maintains consistency even during error conditions.

Integration testing verifies proper interaction between WebSocket components and other system parts. Implement tests that verify proper interaction with databases, external services, and other system components. Consider testing various integration patterns, including event sourcing and message queue integration. Your tests should verify that system components interact correctly across different scenarios.

Performance testing helps ensure acceptable WebSocket performance. Implement tests that measure connection latency, message throughput, and resource utilization. Consider testing various performance scenarios, including high message rates and large payload sizes. Your tests should verify that performance meets your application requirements across different conditions.

Security testing verifies proper protection against various threats. Implement tests that verify proper handling of malformed messages, authentication bypass attempts, and other security concerns. Consider testing various security scenarios, including rate limiting and connection flooding. Your tests should verify that security measures properly protect the system.

Testing tools selection requires careful consideration. Phoenix provides built in testing utilities through Phoenix.ChannelTest, but you might need additional tools for specific testing scenarios. Consider using WebSocket client libraries for external testing and specialized tools for load testing. Choose tools that provide good visibility into test execution and failure analysis.

Test environment setup plays a crucial role in effective WebSocket testing. Implement test environments that closely match your production configuration while remaining isolated and controllable. Consider implementing test helpers that can simplify common testing patterns and reduce test code duplication. Your test environment should support both automated testing and interactive debugging.

Documentation of testing strategies helps maintain testing effectiveness over time. Document your testing approaches, including test coverage goals, testing patterns, and known limitations. Consider maintaining example tests that demonstrate proper testing practices. Your documentation should help team members understand and maintain the testing suite.

Remember that effective WebSocket testing requires ongoing attention and refinement. Regularly review and update your testing strategies as your application evolves. Consider implementing continuous integration pipelines that include comprehensive WebSocket testing. Maintain a balance between test coverage and testing complexity that matches your application needs.

# 40. Testing LiveView Applications

Testing LiveView applications requires a comprehensive approach that differs from traditional web application testing due to the stateful and real time nature of LiveView. The testing strategy must account for both server side state management and client side interactions while ensuring proper handling of live updates and events.

Phoenix provides robust testing utilities specifically designed for LiveView through the Phoenix.LiveViewTest module. This module offers a collection of functions that simulate browser interactions and verify LiveView behavior. The testing utilities allow you to mount LiveViews, simulate user interactions, and verify the resulting state and rendered content.

When testing LiveView applications, start by verifying the initial render state. Your tests should confirm that the LiveView mounts correctly, initializes with the expected state, and renders the proper initial HTML content. Consider testing various mounting scenarios, including different session data and connection parameters. Verify that the initial state matches your expectations and that any necessary data loading occurs correctly.

Event handling represents a crucial aspect of LiveView testing. Implement tests that verify proper handling of various event types, including click events, form submissions, and custom events. Your tests should confirm that events trigger appropriate state updates and that the rendered content reflects these changes. Consider testing both successful event handling and error scenarios to ensure robust behavior.

Form testing requires particular attention in LiveView applications. Verify proper form validation, error handling, and successful submission scenarios. Test various form input types and validation rules to ensure comprehensive coverage. Consider testing form interactions that trigger live updates and verify that the updates occur correctly without full page reloads.

Component testing presents unique challenges in LiveView applications. Test both stateless and stateful components, verifying proper initialization, event handling, and state management. Consider testing component lifecycle events and proper cleanup when components unmount. Verify that components interact correctly with their parent LiveView and maintain proper state isolation.

Hook testing verifies proper interaction between LiveView and custom JavaScript hooks. Implement tests that verify hook initialization, event handling, and proper communication between client and server. Consider testing various hook scenarios, including DOM mutations and custom event handling. Verify that hooks properly clean up resources when components unmount.

Live navigation testing ensures proper handling of live navigation events. Test navigation between different LiveViews, verifying proper state management and content updates. Consider testing both successful navigation scenarios and error cases. Verify that the browser history updates correctly and that back/forward navigation works as expected.

PubSub integration testing verifies proper handling of real time updates. Test subscription management, message broadcasting, and proper state updates in response to PubSub events. Consider testing various subscription patterns and verify that LiveViews properly handle subscription cleanup on dismount.

Connection handling tests verify proper behavior during connection issues. Implement tests that simulate connection drops, reconnections, and various network scenarios. Verify that LiveViews properly handle disconnected states and recover appropriately when connections restore. Consider testing automatic reconnection behavior and proper state recovery.

Performance testing helps ensure acceptable LiveView performance. Measure rendering times, memory usage, and response times for various operations. Consider testing with different data volumes and user interaction patterns. Verify that performance remains acceptable under expected load conditions and that memory usage remains stable over time.

Security testing verifies proper protection against various threats. Test proper handling of user authentication, authorization, and input validation. Consider testing various security scenarios, including cross site scripting protection and proper handling of malicious inputs. Verify that security measures properly protect both server and client components.

Integration testing verifies proper interaction between LiveView and other system components. Test integration with databases, external services, and other application features. Consider testing various integration patterns and verify proper error handling during integration failures. Ensure that LiveViews properly coordinate with other system components.

Test organization plays a crucial role in maintaining a manageable test suite. Structure your tests logically, grouping related tests and maintaining clear separation of concerns. Consider implementing shared test helpers and fixtures to reduce duplication and improve test maintainability. Document testing patterns and conventions to help team members understand and maintain the test suite.

Continuous integration setup ensures consistent testing across development cycles. Configure your CI pipeline to run LiveView tests automatically, including both unit tests and integration tests. Consider implementing visual regression testing for LiveView applications to catch unexpected rendering changes. Ensure that your CI environment properly supports LiveView testing requirements.

Test coverage analysis helps identify areas needing additional testing attention. Use coverage tools to identify untested code paths and interaction patterns. Consider implementing property based testing for complex state management scenarios. Maintain a balance between test coverage and testing complexity that matches your application needs.

Remember that effective LiveView testing requires ongoing refinement as your application evolves. Regularly review and update your testing strategies to address new features and identified issues. Consider implementing automated test generation tools to help maintain comprehensive test coverage. Keep your testing approach aligned with your application's evolving requirements and complexity.

# 41. Integration Testing Real-Time Features

Integration testing real time features requires a comprehensive approach that combines traditional integration testing practices with specialized techniques for verifying asynchronous and real time behavior. These tests ensure that different components of your system work together correctly while handling live updates, WebSocket connections, and state synchronization across multiple clients.

When setting up integration tests for real time features, establish a proper test environment that closely mirrors your production setup. This includes configuring test databases, WebSocket connections, and any external services your application depends on. Consider using Docker containers to create isolated test environments that can be easily replicated and torn down between test runs.

Testing real time chat features presents unique challenges due to the need to verify interactions between multiple connected clients. Create test scenarios that simulate multiple users joining chat rooms, sending messages, and receiving updates. Verify that messages are delivered to all appropriate recipients and that user presence information updates correctly. Test various chat scenarios including private messages, group chats, and message history loading.

Dashboard testing requires verification of live data updates and real time visualizations. Implement tests that simulate data source updates and verify that dashboards reflect changes immediately. Test different update frequencies, data volumes, and visualization types. Verify that dashboard components properly handle concurrent updates and maintain consistent state across multiple viewing clients.

IoT device testing involves verifying proper handling of device connections, data ingestion, and real time monitoring. Create test scenarios that simulate device connections, data transmission, and disconnection events. Verify that your system properly processes device data and triggers appropriate alerts or actions. Test various device states including normal operation, error conditions, and recovery scenarios.

PubSub integration testing verifies proper message distribution across your application. Test different subscription patterns, message formats, and broadcasting scenarios. Verify that subscribers receive appropriate messages and that message ordering maintains consistency. Test subscription cleanup and proper handling of subscription errors or timeouts.

Authentication and authorization testing ensures proper security controls across real time features. Implement tests that verify access controls for WebSocket connections, channel subscriptions, and real time updates. Test various authentication scenarios including token expiration, permission changes, and invalid credentials. Verify that security measures properly protect sensitive real time data.

State synchronization testing verifies proper handling of distributed state across multiple nodes. Create test scenarios that simulate node additions, removals, and network partitions. Verify that state remains consistent across the cluster and that recovery mechanisms work properly. Test various synchronization patterns including leader election, conflict resolution, and state recovery.

Load balancer integration testing ensures proper distribution of WebSocket connections across multiple server instances. Test connection handling, sticky sessions, and failover scenarios. Verify that clients maintain stable connections and receive updates regardless of which server they connect to. Test various load balancing algorithms and connection distribution patterns.

Database integration testing verifies proper handling of real time data persistence and retrieval. Test concurrent data modifications, transaction handling, and consistency requirements. Verify that real time updates properly reflect database state changes. Test various database operations including queries, updates, and deletions under real time conditions.

Message queue integration testing ensures proper handling of asynchronous processing in real time features. Test message publication, consumption, and error handling. Verify that message processing maintains proper ordering and delivery guarantees. Test various queue scenarios including back pressure handling and recovery from processing failures.

External service integration testing verifies proper interaction with third party services in real time contexts. Test API calls, webhooks, and service specific protocols. Verify that your application properly handles service latency, errors, and rate limits. Test various integration patterns including retry mechanisms and circuit breakers.

Error handling testing verifies proper recovery from various failure scenarios. Test network issues, service failures, and system errors. Verify that your application properly handles and recovers from different error conditions. Test error reporting, logging, and monitoring integration under various failure scenarios.

Performance integration testing measures system behavior under realistic loads. Test concurrent connections, message throughput, and resource utilization. Verify that your system maintains acceptable performance levels under expected load conditions. Test various performance scenarios including peak usage, sustained load, and recovery from overload conditions.

Monitoring integration testing ensures proper functionality of system monitoring and alerting. Test metric collection, log aggregation, and alert triggering. Verify that monitoring systems properly track real time system behavior. Test various monitoring scenarios including threshold alerts, trend analysis, and incident response workflows.

Remember to maintain proper test isolation and cleanup between test runs. Implement appropriate setup and teardown procedures that ensure consistent test environments. Consider implementing test helpers and utilities that simplify common testing patterns. Document your integration testing approach and maintain clear test organization to support long term maintenance.

Integration testing of real time features requires ongoing attention as your system evolves. Regularly review and update your integration tests to cover new features and identified edge cases. Consider implementing automated test generation and maintenance tools to help manage test complexity. Keep your integration testing strategy aligned with your system's architecture and reliability requirements.

# 42. Load Testing WebSocket Applications

Load testing WebSocket applications requires a systematic approach to verify system behavior under various load conditions. Understanding how your application performs under stress is crucial for ensuring reliability and scalability in production environments.

Begin by establishing clear performance goals and metrics for your WebSocket application. These might include maximum concurrent connections, message throughput, latency requirements, and resource utilization limits. Document these requirements as they will guide your load testing strategy and help determine success criteria.

When designing load tests for WebSocket applications, create realistic scenarios that mirror actual usage patterns. Consider the typical lifecycle of a WebSocket connection in your application, including initial connection establishment, authentication, message exchange patterns, and disconnection behavior. Model your test scenarios to include a mix of these activities in proportions similar to production usage.

Tools for load testing WebSocket applications differ from traditional HTTP load testing tools. Popular options include Artillery, k6, and custom testing frameworks built with Erlang's Common Test framework. Each tool has its strengths, so evaluate them based on your specific needs. Artillery, for example, excels at testing Phoenix channels and provides excellent reporting capabilities.

Connection establishment testing forms a crucial part of your load testing strategy. Verify how your system handles large numbers of simultaneous connection attempts. Test both successful connections and various failure scenarios. Monitor connection acceptance rates, latency during connection establishment, and system resource utilization during connection spikes.

Message throughput testing verifies your system's capacity to handle high volumes of WebSocket messages. Create test scenarios that simulate different message patterns, sizes, and frequencies. Test both broadcast scenarios where messages go to many clients and targeted messages between specific clients. Monitor message delivery rates, latency, and any message drops or delays.

Long running connection testing evaluates system stability over extended periods. Maintain large numbers of concurrent connections while simulating normal activity patterns. Monitor for memory leaks, connection drops, or degraded performance over time. Test reconnection behavior when connections are lost or servers are restarted.

Resource utilization testing measures how your system uses CPU, memory, network bandwidth, and other resources under load. Monitor both application level metrics and system level resources. Identify bottlenecks and resource constraints that might limit scalability. Test how resource usage scales with increasing numbers of connections and message volumes.

Database interaction testing under load verifies that your persistence layer handles concurrent operations effectively. Simulate realistic patterns of data reads and writes through WebSocket connections. Monitor database performance metrics, connection pool utilization, and query response times under load.

PubSub system testing verifies proper message distribution under high load. Test various subscription patterns and broadcast scenarios with large numbers of subscribers. Monitor message delivery latency and verify that all subscribers receive expected messages. Test how PubSub performance scales across multiple nodes.

Error handling testing under load verifies that your system properly manages failure scenarios at scale. Simulate various error conditions while under load, including network issues, crashed processes, and invalid messages. Verify that error handling mechanisms work correctly and don't cascade into system wide issues.

Authentication and authorization testing under load verifies that security mechanisms perform well at scale. Test authentication processes with many simultaneous connection attempts. Verify that authorization checks maintain acceptable performance under load. Monitor security related metrics and error rates.

Node clustering testing verifies distributed system behavior under load. Test how connection load balances across multiple nodes. Verify that state synchronization mechanisms perform well with high message volumes. Test node failure and recovery scenarios under load.

Client simulation for load testing requires careful consideration. Implement realistic client behavior including connection lifetime, message patterns, and error handling. Consider implementing custom client simulators that better match your application's specific requirements. Test with various client implementations to verify consistent behavior.

Performance monitoring during load tests provides crucial insights. Collect detailed metrics about system behavior under load. Monitor both technical metrics like response times and business metrics like successful transactions. Use monitoring data to identify performance bottlenecks and optimization opportunities.

Load test execution requires careful planning and coordination. Start with basic smoke tests and gradually increase load. Monitor system behavior continuously during tests. Document all test conditions, results, and observations. Maintain detailed records for future comparison and trend analysis.

Results analysis from load tests should be thorough and systematic. Compare results against performance requirements and previous test runs. Identify performance regressions and improvement opportunities. Document findings and recommendations for system optimization.

Regular load testing should be part of your development and maintenance process. Schedule periodic load tests to verify performance hasn't degraded. Update load test scenarios as your application evolves. Maintain automated load testing as part of your continuous integration pipeline where practical.

Remember that load testing WebSocket applications presents unique challenges compared to traditional web applications. Pay special attention to connection management, message delivery patterns, and long term stability. Consider implementing custom metrics and monitoring specific to your WebSocket usage patterns.

# 43. Performance Monitoring

Performance monitoring forms a critical foundation for maintaining healthy real-time applications. A comprehensive monitoring strategy helps detect issues early, optimize system performance, and ensure reliable service delivery for your users.

Start by identifying key metrics that indicate your application's health and performance. For WebSocket applications, these typically include connection counts, message throughput, latency measurements, and resource utilization statistics. Track both system level metrics like CPU usage, memory consumption, and network throughput, as well as application specific metrics such as channel subscription counts, broadcast latencies, and PubSub queue lengths.

The Erlang Virtual Machine (BEAM) provides powerful built in tools for monitoring application performance. Use :observer.start() during development to visualize process relationships, monitor memory usage, and track message queue lengths. The :etop module offers insights into process CPU utilization and scheduling behavior. These tools help identify bottlenecks and understand system behavior under real conditions.

Telemetry plays a crucial role in modern Elixir applications. Phoenix includes telemetry integration out of the box, allowing you to instrument key components of your application. Create custom telemetry events for important business operations and WebSocket interactions. Attach telemetry handlers to aggregate and process these metrics, providing insights into application behavior and performance trends.

Prometheus integration through the Prometheus.ex library enables robust metric collection and visualization. Define custom metrics for WebSocket connections, message rates, and business operations. Use Prometheus's powerful querying capabilities to analyze performance patterns and detect anomalies. Combined with

Grafana for visualization, this creates a powerful monitoring solution for real-time applications.

Application logs provide essential context for performance monitoring. Structure your logging strategy to capture important performance related events without overwhelming storage or impacting system performance. Include correlation IDs in logs to track related events across distributed systems. Consider using log aggregation services to centralize and analyze log data effectively.

Process monitoring requires special attention in Elixir applications. Monitor process counts, message queue lengths, and memory usage patterns. Implement process monitoring strategies using supervisors and process links. Set up alerts for unexpected process terminations or excessive message queue growth that might indicate performance problems.

Memory monitoring helps prevent resource exhaustion and performance degradation. Track both overall system memory usage and per process memory allocation patterns. Monitor garbage collection statistics to identify memory churn issues. Implement memory usage alerts to provide early warning of potential memory leaks or excessive allocation patterns.

Network performance monitoring is crucial for WebSocket applications. Track connection establishment rates, message throughput, and network latency metrics. Monitor for connection drops and reconnection patterns. Implement network quality metrics to understand client connection stability and performance across different network conditions.

Database performance monitoring ensures your persistence layer doesn't become a bottleneck. Track query execution times, connection pool utilization, and transaction throughput. Monitor database size and growth patterns. Implement alerts for slow queries or excessive connection wait times that might impact real-time performance.

PubSub system monitoring helps maintain efficient message distribution. Track subscription counts, broadcast latencies, and message queue lengths. Monitor message delivery patterns across distributed nodes. Implement metrics to verify message delivery reliability and detect potential bottlenecks in the message distribution system.

Distributed system monitoring requires additional consideration. Track node health, distribution protocol metrics, and state synchronization performance. Monitor network partition events and recovery behavior. Implement cluster wide monitoring to understand system behavior across all nodes.

Real time alerting forms an essential part of performance monitoring. Define meaningful alert thresholds based on performance requirements and system capabilities. Implement different alert severity levels for various conditions. Create alert routing rules to ensure notifications reach appropriate team members quickly.

Metric visualization helps understand system behavior and identify trends. Create dashboards that provide both high level system health overview and detailed component metrics. Use time series visualization to identify patterns and correlations. Implement custom visualizations for business specific metrics that matter to your application.

Performance baseline establishment helps detect degradation over time. Regularly collect and analyze performance metrics under normal conditions. Document expected performance ranges for key metrics. Compare current performance against established baselines to identify potential issues early.

Capacity planning relies heavily on performance monitoring data. Use historical metrics to predict resource needs and system scaling requirements. Monitor growth trends in key metrics to anticipate capacity needs. Implement predictive monitoring to provide early warning of approaching capacity limits.

Automated performance monitoring through continuous integration helps catch performance regressions early. Implement performance tests that verify key metrics remain within acceptable ranges. Create automated alerts for significant performance changes between deployments. Maintain historical performance data to track long term trends.

Remember that effective performance monitoring requires ongoing attention and refinement. Regularly review and update monitoring strategies as your application evolves. Maintain documentation about monitoring systems and alert responses. Train team members on monitoring tools and interpretation of key metrics.

Performance monitoring represents a crucial investment in your application's long term health and reliability. Take time to implement comprehensive monitoring from the start of your project. Regular attention to performance metrics helps maintain high quality service and happy users.

# 44. Memory Management

Memory management in Elixir and Phoenix applications requires careful attention to ensure optimal performance and system stability, especially in real time applications handling numerous WebSocket connections. Understanding how the BEAM virtual machine manages memory helps developers make better architectural decisions and avoid common pitfalls.

The BEAM virtual machine employs a sophisticated garbage collection system that operates on a per process basis. This design means that when garbage collection occurs in one process, other processes continue executing without interruption. This characteristic proves particularly valuable in real time applications where consistent responsiveness is crucial. Each process maintains its own heap, and when a process terminates, all its memory is immediately reclaimed, preventing memory leaks at the process level.

Memory in Elixir applications can be broadly categorized into several types. Process heap memory stores the process's own data structures and message queues. Binary memory, managed separately from process heaps, stores larger data chunks like file contents or network payloads. Atom memory contains all registered atoms, which are reference counted but never garbage collected. ETS tables provide a separate memory space for shared state that persists independently of individual processes.

When building real time applications, message passing between processes requires special consideration. While Elixir's message passing is highly efficient, each message is copied between process heaps. For large messages or high frequency communication, this copying can consume significant memory. Consider using ETS tables or other shared memory mechanisms for large datasets that need to be accessed by multiple processes.

Memory fragmentation can occur over time as processes allocate and deallocate memory. The BEAM handles most fragmentation automatically through its garbage collection and memory management systems. However, applications handling large binary data should be particularly careful. Using binary references instead of copying full binary data between processes helps reduce memory usage and fragmentation.

WebSocket connections in Phoenix applications maintain state in dedicated processes. Each connection process consumes memory for its process heap and message queue. When scaling to thousands or millions of connections, memory usage can grow significantly. Implement connection limiting mechanisms and monitor process memory usage to prevent system overload. Consider implementing process hibernation for inactive connections to reduce memory footprint.

Memory leaks in Elixir applications often manifest differently than in other languages. While process isolation prevents many traditional memory leaks, accumulated state in long running processes can cause memory growth over time. Regular monitoring of process memory usage helps identify processes that accumulate state unexpectedly. Implement periodic state cleanup in long running processes to prevent unbounded growth.

ETS tables provide powerful capabilities for shared state but require careful memory management. Monitor table sizes and implement cleanup strategies for temporary data. Consider using table options like read_concurrency and write_concurrency to optimize memory usage based on access patterns. For time series or logging data, implement rotation or archival strategies to prevent unbounded table growth.

Binary data handling requires special attention in real time applications. Large binaries are stored in a separate heap and referenced by processes. When processing large binary messages, use binary pattern matching and streaming approaches to avoid loading entire payloads into process memory. Implement timeout mechanisms for binary processing to prevent resource exhaustion from malformed or malicious data.

Memory allocation patterns can significantly impact application performance. The BEAM's garbage collector optimizes for processes with predictable memory usage patterns. Design processes to maintain relatively stable memory usage rather than frequently allocating and deallocating large amounts of memory. Consider breaking large operations into smaller chunks processed by multiple processes to distribute memory load.

Monitoring memory usage provides essential insights for optimization. Use tools like Observer and process_info to analyze memory usage patterns. Implement custom monitoring for application specific memory metrics. Track memory usage across different operations to identify potential optimization opportunities. Regular memory profiling helps maintain optimal performance as applications evolve.

Process hibernation offers a way to reduce memory usage for inactive processes. Hibernate processes that maintain state but receive infrequent messages. Implement hibernation policies based on activity patterns and system load. Monitor hibernation effectiveness through memory usage metrics and adjust policies accordingly.

Memory optimization often involves tradeoffs between memory usage and computation time. Profile different approaches to find the right balance for your application. Consider using techniques like lazy loading or streaming for large datasets. Implement caching strategies that optimize both memory usage and access patterns.

System configuration impacts memory management effectiveness. Configure VM options like maximum heap size and process limits appropriately for your hardware and workload.

Monitor system memory pressure and implement graceful degradation strategies. Consider using tools like systemd limits to prevent system memory exhaustion.

Distributed systems introduce additional memory management considerations. Coordinate memory usage across nodes to prevent individual node overload. Implement consistent monitoring and alerting across the cluster. Consider memory usage when designing data distribution and replication strategies.

Regular testing under production like conditions helps identify memory issues early. Implement memory focused load tests that simulate real world usage patterns. Monitor memory behavior during extended test runs to identify gradual growth or leaks. Test memory recovery after various failure scenarios.

Memory management strategy should evolve with your application. Regularly review memory usage patterns and optimization opportunities. Update monitoring and alerting thresholds based on operational experience. Maintain documentation about memory management decisions and known patterns.

# 45. CPU Optimization

CPU optimization in real time Phoenix applications requires a deep understanding of both the BEAM virtual machine's characteristics and application specific processing patterns. While Elixir and the BEAM provide excellent concurrency capabilities out of the box, optimizing CPU usage ensures maximum throughput and responsiveness for your real time features.

The BEAM scheduler manages CPU resources across multiple schedulers, typically one per CPU core. Understanding how the scheduler works helps in designing CPU efficient applications. The scheduler distributes processes across available cores, automatically handling load balancing. However, CPU intensive operations in a single process can still impact overall system performance by occupying a scheduler for extended periods.

Process design significantly impacts CPU utilization. Breaking down computationally intensive tasks into smaller units allows better distribution across schedulers. When processing real time data streams or performing complex calculations, consider spawning multiple processes to handle different aspects of the computation. This approach leverages parallel processing capabilities while maintaining system responsiveness.

One common CPU optimization challenge in real time applications involves message processing. While Elixir's message passing is highly efficient, high message volumes can consume significant CPU resources. Implement message batching for high frequency updates to reduce processing overhead. Consider using ETS tables or other shared state mechanisms for data that needs frequent access by multiple processes.

Pattern matching, while powerful, can impact CPU usage when working with complex data structures or large collections. Optimize pattern matching expressions by ordering patterns from most to least specific and avoiding unnecessary matches. When processing large lists or maps, consider using specialized functions like Map.get/3 instead of pattern matching when appropriate.

Real time data processing often involves regular state updates and calculations. Implement caching strategies for computationally expensive operations that don't require real time updates. Use techniques like memoization for frequently accessed calculations with stable inputs. Consider implementing periodic batch processing for operations that don't require immediate execution.

WebSocket connections in Phoenix applications maintain persistent connections that require ongoing CPU resources for message handling and state management. Implement connection pooling and load balancing strategies to distribute connection handling across available cores. Consider using process groups to organize related connections and optimize broadcast operations.

Binary data processing can be CPU intensive, especially when dealing with large payloads or complex transformations. Implement streaming approaches for large binary operations to avoid blocking schedulers. Use binary pattern matching efficiently by avoiding unnecessary copies and transformations. Consider implementing parallel processing for CPU intensive binary operations.

Database operations can significantly impact CPU usage, especially when processing real time updates or performing complex queries. Optimize database queries to minimize CPU overhead on both application and database servers. Implement caching strategies for frequently accessed data. Consider using database specific features like materialized views or computed columns to offload calculations.

Monitoring CPU usage provides essential insights for optimization. Implement detailed monitoring of process CPU usage patterns using tools like Observer and custom metrics. Track CPU utilization across different operations to identify bottlenecks.

Regular profiling helps maintain optimal performance as applications evolve.

The BEAM's preemptive scheduling ensures no single process can completely block the system. However, long running computations can still impact responsiveness. Implement timeouts and circuit breakers for CPU intensive operations. Consider breaking long running calculations into smaller chunks that can be processed incrementally.

Just in time compilation in the BEAM can significantly impact performance. Understanding how code is compiled and optimized helps in writing more efficient functions. Avoid dynamic function calls when possible, as they bypass many compiler optimizations. Consider using module attributes for configuration values that are known at compile time.

CPU optimization often involves tradeoffs between processing time and other resources like memory or network bandwidth. Profile different approaches to find the right balance for your application. Consider implementing adaptive processing strategies that adjust based on system load and available resources.

System configuration can significantly impact CPU utilization. Configure VM options like scheduler count and thread pool sizes appropriately for your hardware. Monitor system CPU pressure and implement graceful degradation strategies. Consider using tools like systemd CPU limits to prevent system overload.

Distributed systems introduce additional CPU optimization considerations. Coordinate processing loads across nodes to prevent individual node overload. Implement consistent monitoring and alerting across the cluster. Consider CPU usage when designing task distribution and failover strategies.

Regular testing under production like conditions helps identify CPU bottlenecks early. Implement CPU focused load tests that simulate real world processing patterns. Monitor CPU behavior during extended test runs to identify gradual performance degradation. Test system behavior under various load conditions and failure scenarios.

CPU optimization strategy should evolve with your application. Regularly review processing patterns and optimization opportunities. Update monitoring and alerting thresholds based on operational experience. Maintain documentation about CPU optimization decisions and known patterns.

Advanced CPU profiling tools can provide detailed insights into application behavior. Use tools like fprof and eprof to analyze function call patterns and execution times. Consider implementing custom profiling for application specific operations. Regular profiling helps identify optimization opportunities and verify improvements.

# 46. Network Optimization

Network optimization in Phoenix applications involves carefully tuning communication patterns and infrastructure to ensure reliable, low latency real time interactions. While Elixir and Phoenix provide excellent networking capabilities by default, optimizing network performance requires understanding both application level protocols and underlying network infrastructure.

WebSocket connections form the foundation of real time features in Phoenix applications. Each connection maintains a persistent TCP connection that consumes network resources. Implementing connection pooling helps manage these resources efficiently. Configure appropriate connection pool sizes based on your application's requirements and available network capacity. Monitor connection pool utilization to identify potential bottlenecks.

Message serialization significantly impacts network performance. Phoenix uses a binary protocol for WebSocket communication that provides efficient message encoding. However, carefully consider payload structure and size. Implement compression for large payloads when appropriate. Structure messages to minimize unnecessary data transmission while maintaining required functionality.

Network latency directly affects real time application responsiveness. Implement client side buffering and debouncing for high frequency updates to reduce network load. Consider using delta updates that transmit only changed data rather than complete state. Implement appropriate retry strategies for failed transmissions that balance reliability with network efficiency.

Load balancing across multiple application nodes requires careful network configuration. Implement sticky sessions when necessary to maintain WebSocket connections. Configure health checks and failover mechanisms appropriate for your infrastructure. Consider network topology when designing node communication patterns.

Phoenix channels provide a powerful abstraction for real time communication. Optimize channel usage by implementing appropriate topic structures that minimize broadcast scope. Consider using presence features efficiently to reduce unnecessary presence related network traffic. Implement proper channel cleanup to prevent resource leaks.

Network monitoring provides essential visibility into application performance. Implement detailed monitoring of network metrics including latency, throughput, and error rates. Track network usage patterns across different features and user behaviors. Regular network performance analysis helps maintain optimal operation.

Content delivery networks can significantly improve network performance for static assets and API endpoints. Configure CDN caching appropriately for your application's needs. Implement cache invalidation strategies that balance freshness with network efficiency. Consider using multiple CDN providers for redundancy when appropriate.

Database connections consume significant network resources in distributed systems. Implement connection pooling for database access with appropriate pool sizes. Consider database replica placement to minimize network latency for read operations. Implement efficient query patterns that minimize network round trips.

SSL/TLS configuration significantly impacts network performance. Implement appropriate cipher suites and protocol versions for your security requirements. Configure session caching and ticket mechanisms to reduce handshake overhead. Consider implementing HTTP/2 for improved connection efficiency.

Network partitions require careful handling in distributed systems. Implement appropriate partition detection mechanisms. Design failure modes that maintain system stability during network issues. Consider implementing circuit breakers for external service dependencies.

Message queues often play crucial roles in distributed systems. Configure queue clients with appropriate network timeouts and retry strategies. Implement efficient message routing patterns that minimize network overhead. Consider message batch processing when appropriate.

DNS configuration affects system reliability and performance. Implement appropriate DNS caching and resolution strategies. Consider using multiple DNS providers for redundancy. Configure appropriate TTL values for DNS records based on your deployment patterns.

Network security measures can impact performance. Implement rate limiting and throttling mechanisms that protect systems while maintaining responsiveness. Configure firewall rules appropriately for your application's communication patterns. Consider implementing network level access controls when appropriate.

WebSocket compression provides opportunities for reducing network bandwidth usage. Configure compression options based on message patterns and client capabilities. Consider implementing custom compression schemes for application specific data formats. Monitor compression effectiveness across different types of payloads.

Inter node communication in distributed systems requires careful optimization. Implement efficient serialization formats for node communication. Consider network topology when designing distributed algorithms. Implement appropriate network failure handling mechanisms.

Client network conditions significantly impact user experience. Implement graceful degradation for poor network conditions.

Consider implementing offline capabilities when appropriate. Design user interfaces that provide appropriate feedback during network issues.

Network capacity planning ensures sustainable system growth. Monitor network resource utilization trends. Implement appropriate scaling strategies based on network usage patterns. Consider network requirements when planning system expansions.

Regular network performance testing helps maintain optimal operation. Implement network focused load tests that simulate real world conditions. Monitor network behavior during extended test runs. Test system behavior under various network conditions and failure scenarios.

Network optimization strategy should evolve with your application. Regularly review network usage patterns and optimization opportunities. Update monitoring and alerting thresholds based on operational experience. Maintain documentation about network optimization decisions and known patterns.

The increasing adoption of edge computing introduces additional network optimization considerations. Design appropriate data distribution patterns for edge deployments. Consider network latency when planning edge processing strategies. Implement efficient synchronization mechanisms between edge nodes and central systems.

# 47. Deployment Strategies

Deploying real time Phoenix applications requires careful consideration of various deployment strategies to ensure reliability, scalability, and maintainable operations. A well planned deployment approach helps maintain system stability while enabling continuous delivery of new features and improvements.

Release builds form a fundamental part of Phoenix deployment strategy. Implementing proper release configuration ensures reliable application packaging and deployment. Configure release settings appropriate for your deployment environment including runtime configuration management. Consider implementing automated release verification processes to catch potential issues early.

Deployment automation helps maintain consistent and reliable processes. Implement automated deployment pipelines that include appropriate testing and verification steps. Consider using infrastructure as code approaches to maintain deployment consistency. Implement appropriate rollback capabilities for deployment issues.

Blue green deployment patterns provide reliable update mechanisms with minimal downtime. Implement appropriate routing and load balancer configuration to support seamless transitions. Consider database migration strategies compatible with blue green deployments. Implement proper health check mechanisms to verify deployment success.

Container based deployments offer flexibility and consistency across environments. Implement appropriate container configuration including resource limits and health checks. Consider implementing container orchestration appropriate for your scale requirements. Design container networking appropriate for your application architecture.

Configuration management significantly impacts deployment reliability. Implement secure configuration management appropriate for sensitive settings. Consider using runtime configuration for values that need operational flexibility. Implement appropriate configuration validation mechanisms.

Database deployment strategy requires careful planning to maintain data integrity. Implement appropriate database migration processes including rollback capabilities. Consider implementing zero downtime migration patterns when appropriate. Design deployment processes that maintain database consistency.

Asset compilation and delivery needs careful consideration in Phoenix applications. Implement appropriate asset build and optimization processes. Consider implementing CDN integration for asset delivery. Design asset versioning strategies that support efficient caching.

Environment specific configuration requires careful management. Implement appropriate configuration isolation between environments. Consider implementing configuration validation processes. Design deployment processes that maintain proper environment separation.

Monitoring and logging infrastructure needs appropriate deployment consideration. Implement monitoring deployment appropriate for your operational requirements. Consider implementing centralized logging infrastructure. Design appropriate alerting configuration deployment.

Deployment security requires careful attention throughout the process. Implement appropriate access controls for deployment processes. Consider implementing deployment audit logging. Design secure credential management for deployment processes.

Scale out deployments require careful planning for distributed systems. Implement appropriate node discovery and communication configuration. Consider implementing automated scale out processes. Design deployment processes that maintain system stability during scaling.

Database deployment patterns significantly impact system reliability. Implement appropriate replica deployment and configuration. Consider implementing database failover configuration. Design deployment processes that maintain database availability.

Load balancer configuration forms a crucial part of deployment strategy. Implement appropriate health check and routing configuration. Consider implementing SSL termination configuration. Design load balancer updates that maintain system availability.

Deployment monitoring provides essential operational visibility. Implement appropriate deployment success metrics. Consider implementing deployment performance monitoring. Design monitoring that provides early warning of deployment issues.

Rollback capabilities provide essential safety mechanisms. Implement appropriate application state rollback processes. Consider implementing database rollback capabilities. Design rollback processes that maintain system consistency.

Cache warming strategies help maintain system performance during deployments. Implement appropriate cache population processes. Consider implementing graduated traffic transition. Design cache warming that minimizes performance impact.

Queue processing requires careful handling during deployments. Implement appropriate message handling during deployment transitions. Consider implementing queue drain processes when needed. Design deployment processes that maintain message processing consistency.

Deployment documentation helps maintain operational knowledge. Implement appropriate deployment process documentation. Consider implementing deployment runbook maintenance. Design documentation that supports operational requirements.

Third party service integration requires careful deployment consideration. Implement appropriate service configuration management. Consider implementing service dependency verification. Design deployment processes that maintain service integration reliability.

Database connection management needs careful handling during deployments. Implement appropriate connection pool management during transitions. Consider implementing connection draining processes. Design deployment processes that maintain connection stability.

Asset versioning strategy significantly impacts deployment reliability. Implement appropriate asset version management. Consider implementing cache busting mechanisms. Design asset deployment that maintains user experience.

Deployment metrics provide essential operational insights. Implement appropriate deployment success tracking. Consider implementing deployment performance monitoring. Design metrics that support continuous improvement.

Regular deployment testing helps maintain reliable processes. Implement deployment focused test environments. Consider implementing deployment simulation capabilities. Design testing that verifies deployment reliability.

Deployment strategy should evolve with operational experience. Regularly review deployment patterns and improvement opportunities. Update deployment processes based on lessons learned. Maintain documentation about deployment decisions and known patterns.

The increasing complexity of modern applications requires careful attention to deployment strategy. Regular review and refinement of deployment processes helps maintain system reliability while enabling efficient delivery of new features and improvements.

# 48. Container Orchestration

Container orchestration plays a vital role in managing and scaling real time Phoenix applications effectively. As applications grow in complexity and scale, proper orchestration becomes essential for maintaining reliability and operational efficiency.

Kubernetes has emerged as the leading container orchestration platform, offering robust capabilities for Phoenix application deployment. When implementing Kubernetes orchestration, careful consideration must be given to pod configuration and resource allocation. Define appropriate resource requests and limits to ensure efficient cluster utilization. Configure liveness and readiness probes specific to Phoenix application requirements to maintain system health.

StatefulSet configurations become particularly important when managing distributed Phoenix applications. Proper configuration ensures stable network identities and storage for distributed nodes. Implement appropriate headless services to enable direct pod to pod communication. Consider using pod anti affinity rules to distribute nodes across failure domains.

Service discovery and DNS configuration significantly impact distributed system reliability. Implement appropriate service definitions to enable reliable pod communication. Configure proper DNS policies to support node discovery in distributed scenarios. Consider implementing custom service discovery patterns when needed for specific requirements.

Persistent storage management requires careful consideration in containerized environments. Implement appropriate volume claims and storage classes for database and file storage needs. Consider implementing backup and restore processes compatible with container orchestration. Design storage configuration that maintains data durability during pod rescheduling.

Network policy configuration becomes crucial for securing containerized applications. Implement appropriate pod to pod communication policies. Configure proper ingress and egress rules to control external communication. Consider implementing network segmentation for enhanced security.

Secret management needs special attention in orchestrated environments. Implement secure secret storage and distribution mechanisms. Configure appropriate secret mounting and rotation capabilities. Consider implementing external secret management integration when needed.

Configuration management should leverage orchestration platform capabilities. Implement ConfigMap resources for non sensitive configuration. Configure appropriate configuration update mechanisms. Consider implementing dynamic configuration reloading when needed.

Load balancing configuration becomes more complex in orchestrated environments. Implement appropriate service type configuration for external access. Configure proper session affinity when needed for WebSocket connections. Consider implementing custom load balancing logic for specific requirements.

Resource quota management helps maintain cluster stability. Implement appropriate namespace resource quotas. Configure proper limit ranges for pods and containers. Consider implementing custom resource metrics for application specific scaling.

Horizontal pod autoscaling provides automated scaling capabilities. Implement appropriate scaling metrics and thresholds. Configure proper scaling behavior including cooldown periods. Consider implementing custom metrics adapters for application specific scaling.

Rolling update configuration significantly impacts deployment reliability. Implement appropriate update strategies including maximum unavailable pods. Configure proper readiness probe settings to control update progression. Consider implementing canary deployment patterns for critical updates.

Monitoring and logging infrastructure needs appropriate orchestration support. Implement centralized logging collection compatible with container environments. Configure appropriate monitoring agent deployment. Consider implementing custom metrics collection for application specific monitoring.

Service mesh integration can enhance application networking capabilities. Implement appropriate proxy configuration for enhanced traffic control. Configure proper circuit breaking and retry logic. Consider implementing advanced routing patterns when needed.

Node affinity and anti affinity rules help optimize pod placement. Implement appropriate node selection rules based on hardware requirements. Configure proper pod distribution for reliability. Consider implementing custom scheduling rules for specific requirements.

Init container configuration helps manage startup dependencies. Implement appropriate initialization processes including database migration. Configure proper startup order for distributed systems. Consider implementing custom health check logic during initialization.

Pod disruption budgets help maintain system availability during maintenance. Implement appropriate availability constraints for critical services. Configure proper eviction policies during node maintenance. Consider implementing custom availability rules for specific requirements.

Network ingress configuration requires careful attention. Implement appropriate routing rules for external access. Configure proper SSL termination and certificate management. Consider implementing custom routing logic for specific requirements.

Priority and preemption configuration helps maintain critical service availability. Implement appropriate pod priority classes. Configure proper preemption policies for resource contention. Consider implementing custom priority rules for specific requirements.

Container image management significantly impacts deployment reliability. Implement appropriate image tagging and versioning strategies. Configure proper image pull policies and registry access. Consider implementing custom image lifecycle management.

The complexity of container orchestration requires ongoing attention to operational patterns and practices. Regular review of orchestration configuration helps maintain system reliability while enabling efficient scaling and management of Phoenix applications. As orchestration platforms evolve, staying current with best practices and new capabilities helps maximize the benefits of containerized deployment.

# 49. Scaling with Kubernetes

Scaling Phoenix applications with Kubernetes requires careful planning and implementation of various strategies to ensure optimal performance and reliability. The distributed nature of Phoenix applications, particularly those leveraging WebSocket connections and real time features, presents unique challenges when deploying on Kubernetes infrastructure.

Resource allocation plays a critical role in Kubernetes scaling strategies. When scaling Phoenix applications, proper configuration of resource requests and limits becomes essential. Applications handling WebSocket connections require careful consideration of memory allocation, as each connection maintains state. Configure horizontal pod autoscaling based on connection metrics rather than just CPU utilization to ensure proper scaling behavior.

Pod affinity and topology spread constraints help optimize WebSocket connection distribution. Implementing proper pod affinity rules ensures connections are distributed effectively across nodes while maintaining session affinity when required. This becomes particularly important when dealing with distributed Phoenix applications using Phoenix.PubSub for communication between nodes.

Connection management requires special consideration when scaling. Implementing proper connection draining during pod termination ensures graceful handling of WebSocket connections. Configure appropriate termination grace periods to allow existing connections to complete or migrate. Consider implementing custom connection management logic through Kubernetes lifecycle hooks.

State synchronization between pods becomes crucial when scaling distributed Phoenix applications. Implementing proper EPMD configuration ensures reliable communication between Erlang nodes. Configure appropriate DNS settings to support node discovery and clustering. Consider implementing custom service discovery patterns for specific clustering requirements.

Load balancing configuration significantly impacts WebSocket connection handling. Implementing proper service annotations ensures effective traffic distribution. Configure appropriate session affinity settings to maintain WebSocket connection stability. Consider implementing custom load balancing logic through ingress controllers when needed.

Database connection pooling requires careful configuration when scaling. Implementing appropriate pool sizing per pod ensures efficient database utilization. Configure proper connection limits to prevent database overload during scaling events. Consider implementing connection pooling patterns specific to your database technology.

Memory management becomes increasingly important at scale. Implementing appropriate garbage collection settings helps maintain consistent performance. Configure proper memory limits to prevent out of memory scenarios. Consider implementing custom memory management strategies through application configuration.

Monitoring and metrics collection needs to scale with the application. Implementing proper metric aggregation ensures visibility into system performance. Configure appropriate metric collection intervals to balance information quality with system impact. Consider implementing custom metrics specific to your application's scaling behavior.

Log management requires attention when scaling. Implementing centralized logging helps maintain visibility across pods. Configure appropriate log rotation and retention policies to manage storage requirements. Consider implementing structured logging patterns to facilitate log analysis at scale.

Network policy configuration becomes crucial at scale. Implementing appropriate pod to pod communication rules ensures proper isolation. Configure proper ingress and egress policies to control external communication. Consider implementing network segmentation for enhanced security at scale.

Certificate management requires automation when scaling. Implementing proper certificate distribution ensures secure communication. Configure appropriate certificate rotation mechanisms to maintain security. Consider implementing external certificate management integration for enhanced automation.

Configuration management needs to support scaling requirements. Implementing proper ConfigMap and Secret distribution ensures consistent configuration. Configure appropriate update mechanisms to handle configuration changes at scale. Consider implementing dynamic configuration reloading when needed.

Backup and restore processes need to scale appropriately. Implementing proper backup scheduling ensures data protection at scale. Configure appropriate backup retention policies to manage storage requirements. Consider implementing distributed backup strategies for large scale deployments.

Health checking becomes more complex at scale. Implementing appropriate liveness and readiness probes ensures proper pod lifecycle management. Configure proper probe timing to prevent false positives during scaling events. Consider implementing custom health check logic for specific requirements.

Resource quota management helps maintain cluster stability at scale. Implementing appropriate namespace quotas prevents resource exhaustion. Configure proper limit ranges to ensure consistent pod sizing. Consider implementing custom resource metrics for application specific scaling.

Deployment strategies need to account for scaling requirements. Implementing appropriate rolling update configurations ensures reliable deployments at scale. Configure proper deployment parameters to maintain system stability during updates. Consider implementing canary deployment patterns for critical changes.

Performance optimization becomes increasingly important at scale. Implementing proper resource utilization helps maintain consistent performance. Configure appropriate scaling thresholds based on application metrics. Consider implementing custom optimization strategies for specific workload patterns.

Security configuration needs to scale appropriately. Implementing proper security policies ensures consistent protection. Configure appropriate security context constraints for pods. Consider implementing additional security layers for sensitive workloads.

The successful scaling of Phoenix applications on Kubernetes requires ongoing attention to these various aspects. Regular review and adjustment of scaling configuration helps maintain optimal performance while ensuring reliable operation at scale. As applications grow, staying current with Kubernetes best practices and capabilities helps maximize scaling effectiveness.

# 50. Cloud Provider Integration

Cloud provider integration represents a crucial aspect of deploying and managing real time Phoenix applications at scale. Modern cloud platforms offer numerous services and features that can enhance the capabilities of Phoenix applications while simplifying operational complexity.

When integrating with cloud providers, storage services become a fundamental consideration. Cloud object storage services provide scalable solutions for handling user generated content, application assets, and backup data. Implementing proper storage integration requires careful consideration of access patterns and performance requirements. Cloud providers typically offer multiple storage tiers, allowing optimization of cost and performance based on access frequency.

Authentication and authorization services provided by cloud platforms can enhance application security. Many providers offer managed identity services that integrate well with Phoenix applications. These services can handle user authentication, role based access control, and token management. Implementing proper integration with these services requires careful consideration of security requirements and compliance standards.

Message queuing services offered by cloud providers can enhance application scalability. These services integrate well with Phoenix applications, particularly for handling asynchronous processing and event driven architectures. Proper implementation requires consideration of message delivery guarantees, throughput requirements, and failure handling mechanisms. Cloud providers typically offer multiple queuing options with different performance characteristics and cost models.

Managed database services simplify database operations while providing scalability and reliability. Cloud providers offer various database options that work well with Phoenix applications. Implementing proper database integration requires consideration of connection management, backup strategies, and scaling capabilities. Many providers offer features like automatic scaling and failover that can enhance application reliability.

Content delivery networks provided by cloud platforms can improve application performance. These services integrate well with Phoenix applications, particularly for serving static assets and handling global traffic distribution. Proper implementation requires consideration of caching strategies, invalidation mechanisms, and edge computing capabilities. Cloud providers typically offer various CDN features that can be leveraged based on specific requirements.

Monitoring and logging services offered by cloud providers enhance operational visibility. These services integrate well with Phoenix applications, providing insights into application performance and behavior. Implementing proper monitoring integration requires consideration of metric collection, log aggregation, and alerting mechanisms. Cloud providers often offer advanced analytics and visualization capabilities that can aid in troubleshooting and optimization.

Container registry services simplify deployment and management of containerized applications. Cloud providers offer reliable registry services that integrate well with container orchestration platforms. Implementing proper registry integration requires consideration of access control, image scanning, and vulnerability management. Many providers offer features like automatic container scanning and policy enforcement.

Load balancing services provided by cloud platforms enhance application availability. These services integrate well with Phoenix applications, particularly for handling WebSocket connections and distributed architectures. Proper implementation requires consideration of session affinity, SSL termination, and health checking mechanisms. Cloud providers typically offer advanced load balancing features that can be customized based on specific requirements.

DNS services offered by cloud providers simplify domain management and traffic routing. These services integrate well with Phoenix applications, providing capabilities for global traffic distribution and failover. Implementing proper DNS integration requires consideration of routing policies, health checking, and failover mechanisms. Many providers offer features like geolocation based routing and traffic management policies.

Key management services enhance application security through proper secret management. Cloud providers offer managed services for handling encryption keys and sensitive configuration. Implementing proper key management integration requires consideration of access control, rotation policies, and audit requirements. These services often provide features like automatic key rotation and access logging.

Cache services provided by cloud platforms can improve application performance. These services integrate well with Phoenix applications, particularly for distributed caching scenarios. Proper implementation requires consideration of cache invalidation, consistency requirements, and failure handling. Cloud providers typically offer various caching options with different performance characteristics.

Queue processing services simplify handling of background jobs and scheduled tasks. These services integrate well with Phoenix applications, providing reliable job execution and scheduling capabilities. Implementing proper queue processing integration requires consideration of job prioritization, retry mechanisms, and monitoring requirements. Many providers offer features like automatic scaling and dead letter queues.

Email services offered by cloud providers simplify handling of application notifications. These services integrate well with Phoenix applications, providing reliable email delivery and tracking capabilities. Proper implementation requires consideration of delivery rates, template management, and bounce handling. Cloud providers typically offer features like email analytics and reputation management.

The successful integration of cloud provider services requires ongoing attention to security, performance, and cost optimization. Regular review of service usage and configuration helps maintain optimal operation while controlling costs. As applications evolve, staying current with cloud provider capabilities and best practices helps maximize the benefits of cloud integration.

# 51. Monitoring in Production

Monitoring production systems requires a comprehensive approach that encompasses multiple layers of observability and proactive maintenance. For real time Phoenix applications, effective monitoring becomes even more critical due to the dynamic nature of WebSocket connections and live updates.

Application metrics form the foundation of production monitoring. Key metrics for Phoenix applications include request throughput, response times, WebSocket connection counts, and channel subscription statistics. These metrics provide insights into application performance and user engagement patterns. Implementing proper metric collection requires careful consideration of sampling rates and storage requirements to balance visibility with resource utilization.

Error tracking becomes essential for maintaining application reliability. Production environments should implement robust error tracking that captures both expected and unexpected failures. This includes monitoring for failed WebSocket connections, channel crashes, and process terminations. Error tracking should provide context around failures, including user information, environment details, and stack traces when appropriate.

System level monitoring provides visibility into the underlying infrastructure. This includes tracking CPU usage, memory utilization, network performance, and disk metrics. For Phoenix applications, particular attention should be paid to BEAM VM metrics such as process counts, memory distribution, and scheduler utilization. Understanding these metrics helps identify potential bottlenecks and capacity constraints.

Database monitoring ensures optimal data layer performance. This includes tracking query execution times, connection pool utilization, and index effectiveness. For real time applications, monitoring write throughput and replication lag becomes particularly important. Implementation should include alerting for slow queries and connection pool exhaustion.

Network monitoring is crucial for WebSocket based applications. This includes tracking connection establishment times, message latency, and protocol upgrades. Proper network monitoring helps identify connectivity issues and potential denial of service attempts. Implementation should consider both client side and server side metrics to provide complete visibility.

Process monitoring within the BEAM VM requires special attention. This includes tracking process counts, message queue lengths, and garbage collection metrics. For Phoenix applications, monitoring GenServer behavior and supervision tree health becomes essential. Implementation should include alerting for process crashes and supervision tree restarts.

Cache monitoring helps optimize application performance. This includes tracking cache hit rates, eviction patterns, and memory usage. For distributed applications, monitoring cache consistency and replication status becomes important. Implementation should consider both application level and infrastructure level caching metrics.

Message queue monitoring ensures reliable event processing. This includes tracking queue depths, processing rates, and dead letter queues. For real time applications, monitoring message ordering and delivery guarantees becomes crucial. Implementation should include alerting for queue backlog and processing delays.

User experience monitoring provides insights into application usability. This includes tracking page load times, WebSocket connection stability, and client side errors. Implementation should consider both synthetic monitoring and real user monitoring approaches to provide comprehensive visibility.

Security monitoring helps protect against threats and vulnerabilities. This includes tracking authentication attempts, rate limit violations, and suspicious patterns. For WebSocket applications, monitoring connection patterns and message content becomes particularly important. Implementation should include automated responses to potential security threats.

Performance monitoring focuses on application responsiveness. This includes tracking response time distributions, resource utilization patterns, and bottlenecks. For LiveView applications, monitoring render times and client side performance becomes crucial. Implementation should include both real time monitoring and historical trend analysis.

Dependency monitoring ensures reliable external service integration. This includes tracking API response times, error rates, and service availability. For distributed systems, monitoring service discovery and circuit breaker status becomes important. Implementation should include alerting for dependency failures and degraded performance.

Log monitoring provides contextual information about application behavior. This includes tracking error patterns, user activities, and system events. For real time applications, monitoring WebSocket related logs becomes particularly important. Implementation should include log aggregation and analysis capabilities.

Alerting strategies must be carefully designed to avoid alert fatigue while ensuring critical issues are addressed. This includes defining appropriate thresholds, implementing escalation policies, and providing context for troubleshooting. Implementation should consider both automated responses and human notification requirements.

Visualization tools help understand system behavior and identify trends. This includes dashboards for real time metrics, historical analysis tools, and correlation capabilities. For Phoenix applications, visualizing WebSocket connections and channel metrics becomes particularly valuable. Implementation should provide both high level overviews and detailed drill down capabilities.

The success of production monitoring depends on regular review and refinement of monitoring strategies. This includes adjusting thresholds, updating alerting policies, and improving visualization tools. As applications evolve, monitoring requirements should be regularly reassessed to ensure continued effectiveness.

# 52. Logging Best Practices

Effective logging practices form a crucial foundation for maintaining and troubleshooting real time Phoenix applications in production environments. A well designed logging strategy provides visibility into application behavior while managing storage and performance considerations.

Structured logging should be implemented throughout the application to ensure consistent and searchable log entries. Each log entry should include essential context such as timestamp, environment, process ID, and correlation identifiers. For Phoenix applications, including request IDs and user context helps trace activities across distributed systems.

Log levels must be carefully chosen to balance visibility with performance. Debug logs provide detailed information for development but should be limited in production. Info level logs capture normal application events, while warn and error levels indicate increasing severity. Critical logs should be reserved for severe issues requiring immediate attention.

WebSocket specific logging requires special consideration in Phoenix applications. Connection establishment, disconnections, and channel events should be logged with appropriate context. Including client information and connection duration helps understand usage patterns. Message payload logging should be carefully controlled to prevent sensitive data exposure.

Error logging demands particular attention to provide sufficient context for troubleshooting. Stack traces should be captured along with relevant application state. For LiveView applications, both server side and client side errors need proper logging. Implementation should include error categorization and correlation capabilities.

Performance logging helps identify bottlenecks and optimization opportunities. Response times, database queries, and resource utilization should be logged at appropriate intervals. For real time applications, logging message processing times and channel broadcast metrics becomes important. Care must be taken to prevent logging itself from impacting performance.

Security event logging provides audit trails and threat detection capabilities. Authentication attempts, authorization failures, and suspicious activities should be thoroughly logged. For WebSocket applications, logging connection patterns and rate limit violations becomes crucial. Implementation must ensure secure handling of sensitive log data.

Log rotation and retention policies must be carefully designed to manage storage requirements. This includes implementing appropriate file size limits and retention periods. For distributed systems, log shipping and centralized storage become important considerations. Implementation should include monitoring of log storage utilization.

Log aggregation strategies need to account for distributed system complexity. This includes collecting logs from multiple nodes and services while maintaining proper ordering. For Phoenix applications, correlating logs across WebSocket connections and channels becomes essential. Implementation should consider both real time aggregation and batch processing approaches.

Logging middleware can provide consistent handling across application components. This includes request logging, error capturing, and performance monitoring. For Phoenix applications, implementing custom logging plugs helps ensure comprehensive coverage. Care must be taken to maintain middleware performance and reliability.

Development environment logging often differs from production requirements. This includes more verbose logging levels and additional context for debugging. Implementation should provide configuration options to adjust logging behavior across environments. Care must be taken to prevent sensitive information in development logs.

Log analysis tools help extract insights from logging data. This includes search capabilities, visualization tools, and alerting integration. For real time applications, analyzing WebSocket connection patterns and error trends becomes valuable. Implementation should balance analysis capabilities with resource requirements.

Logging best practices include avoiding sensitive data exposure in logs. This includes personally identifiable information, credentials, and business sensitive data. For Phoenix applications, particular attention must be paid to WebSocket message content. Implementation should include data masking and filtering capabilities.

Performance impact of logging must be carefully managed. This includes optimizing log writing operations and managing log buffer sizes. For high throughput applications, asynchronous logging becomes particularly important. Implementation should include monitoring of logging system performance.

Log format standardization helps ensure consistent processing and analysis. This includes defining structured formats and required fields. For distributed systems, maintaining format consistency across services becomes crucial. Implementation should consider both human readability and machine processing requirements.

Integration with external logging services requires careful consideration. This includes managing API reliability and handling connection failures. For cloud deployments, utilizing provider specific logging services may offer advantages. Implementation should include fallback mechanisms for external service failures.

Compliance requirements often influence logging strategies. This includes retention periods, access controls, and audit capabilities. For regulated industries, logging requirements may be particularly stringent. Implementation must ensure compliance while maintaining system performance.

Log based metrics provide valuable insights into application behavior. This includes error rates, activity patterns, and performance trends. For real time applications, analyzing WebSocket metrics through logs becomes valuable. Implementation should balance metric extraction with logging system performance.

Testing logging implementation ensures reliable operation in production. This includes verifying log capture, rotation, and analysis capabilities. For distributed systems, testing log aggregation and correlation becomes important. Implementation should include regular validation of logging functionality.

Documentation of logging practices helps maintain consistent implementation. This includes logging conventions, configuration options, and analysis procedures. For team environments, establishing clear logging guidelines becomes crucial. Regular review and updates of documentation help ensure continued effectiveness.

# 53. Error Handling and Recovery

Error handling and recovery strategies form a critical aspect of building robust real time Phoenix applications. A comprehensive error handling approach helps maintain system stability and provides graceful degradation when issues occur.

Application errors must be properly categorized to enable appropriate handling strategies. This includes distinguishing between expected errors like validation failures and unexpected system errors. For Phoenix applications, handling both synchronous and asynchronous errors becomes crucial. Implementation should provide meaningful error responses while maintaining system stability.

WebSocket specific error handling requires particular attention in Phoenix applications. Connection failures, protocol errors, and message handling issues need proper management. This includes implementing reconnection strategies and maintaining session state during disruptions. Error handling should account for both client side and server side failure scenarios.

LiveView error handling presents unique challenges due to its stateful nature. Server crashes, network interruptions, and state synchronization failures need careful handling. Implementation should provide graceful degradation of functionality while attempting recovery. User experience considerations become particularly important in error scenarios.

Process supervision strategies play a key role in error recovery. This includes defining appropriate restart strategies and handling process dependencies. For distributed systems, coordinating recovery across nodes becomes essential. Implementation should balance quick recovery with preventing cascading failures.

Database error handling must account for various failure scenarios. This includes connection losses, deadlocks, and constraint violations. For real time applications, maintaining data consistency during errors becomes crucial. Implementation should include proper transaction management and rollback capabilities.

Memory related errors require careful handling to prevent system instability. This includes managing process memory limits and handling out of memory conditions. For long running connections, monitoring and managing memory usage becomes essential. Implementation should include memory cleanup during error recovery.

Network error handling must address both temporary and persistent failures. This includes implementing proper timeouts and handling partial failures. For distributed systems, network partition scenarios need particular attention. Implementation should maintain system availability while attempting recovery.

Error reporting requires careful design to provide actionable information. This includes capturing relevant context and maintaining error history. For production systems, error aggregation and analysis capabilities become important. Implementation should balance detail with system performance impact.

User facing error handling must provide appropriate feedback while maintaining security. This includes sanitizing error messages and preventing information leakage. For WebSocket applications, maintaining connection state during errors becomes important. Implementation should guide users through recovery steps when appropriate.

Background job error handling requires specific strategies. This includes managing retry attempts and handling permanent failures. For real time processing, maintaining event ordering during recovery becomes crucial. Implementation should prevent data loss while managing system resources.

Cache error handling must address both local and distributed scenarios. This includes handling cache inconsistencies and recovery procedures. For real time applications, maintaining cache freshness during errors becomes important. Implementation should include cache revalidation strategies.

Message queue error handling requires robust retry mechanisms. This includes managing failed deliveries and handling queue overflows. For distributed systems, maintaining message ordering during recovery becomes essential. Implementation should prevent message loss while managing system resources.

Error monitoring systems must provide comprehensive visibility. This includes real time alerting and trend analysis capabilities. For production systems, correlating errors across components becomes crucial. Implementation should balance monitoring detail with system impact.

Recovery procedures must be properly tested to ensure effectiveness. This includes simulating various failure scenarios and validating recovery behavior. For distributed systems, testing network partition recovery becomes particularly important. Implementation should include regular validation of recovery mechanisms.

Performance degradation handling requires careful threshold management. This includes implementing circuit breakers and throttling mechanisms. For real time applications, maintaining minimum service levels becomes crucial. Implementation should prevent complete system failure during overload.

Security error handling demands particular attention to prevent vulnerabilities. This includes managing authentication failures and detecting attack patterns. For WebSocket applications, handling connection flooding becomes important. Implementation should maintain security while enabling legitimate recovery attempts.

Configuration error handling must prevent system instability. This includes validating configuration changes and providing fallback options. For distributed systems, maintaining configuration consistency becomes crucial. Implementation should enable recovery from misconfiguration scenarios.

External service error handling requires proper isolation and fallback strategies. This includes managing timeouts and implementing circuit breakers. For real time applications, maintaining responsiveness during external failures becomes important. Implementation should provide degraded functionality when necessary.

Error recovery metrics help optimize handling strategies. This includes tracking recovery success rates and performance impact. For production systems, analyzing error patterns becomes valuable. Implementation should enable continuous improvement of recovery mechanisms.

Documentation of error handling procedures supports effective operation. This includes error response guides and recovery playbooks. For team environments, establishing clear incident response processes becomes crucial. Regular review and updates ensure continued effectiveness of error handling strategies.

# 54. Security Best Practices

Security best practices form a critical foundation for building reliable and trustworthy real time Phoenix applications. A comprehensive security approach must address multiple layers of the application stack while maintaining performance and scalability.

Authentication and authorization require careful implementation in real time applications. Token based authentication often works well for WebSocket connections, providing a balance of security and performance. The authentication mechanism should support session management while preventing unauthorized access attempts. Tokens should be properly scoped and include appropriate expiration policies.

Data encryption plays a vital role in protecting sensitive information. All WebSocket communications should use TLS encryption to prevent man in the middle attacks. Additionally, sensitive data stored within the application should use appropriate encryption at rest. Key management becomes particularly important in distributed systems where encryption keys must be securely shared across nodes.

Input validation must be rigorously implemented throughout the application. This includes validating both initial connection parameters and ongoing message content. For LiveView applications, server side validation becomes crucial as client side checks can be bypassed. Validation should account for various attack vectors including injection attempts and malformed data.

Rate limiting and throttling mechanisms help prevent resource exhaustion attacks. This includes implementing connection limits, message rate controls, and resource usage boundaries. For distributed systems, coordination of rate limiting across nodes becomes important. The implementation should balance security with legitimate high volume usage patterns.

Session management requires careful attention to security details. This includes proper session initialization, secure storage of session data, and appropriate cleanup procedures. For WebSocket connections, handling session expiration and renewal becomes particularly important. The implementation should prevent session hijacking while maintaining user experience.

Cross Site Scripting (XSS) prevention becomes crucial in real time applications. This includes proper escaping of dynamic content and validation of user generated data. For LiveView applications, careful handling of HTML injection vectors becomes essential. The implementation should prevent script injection while maintaining interactive functionality.

Cross Site Request Forgery (CSRF) protection needs careful consideration. This includes implementing appropriate tokens and origin validation. For WebSocket connections, initial handshake protection becomes particularly important. The implementation should prevent unauthorized cross origin requests while supporting legitimate integrations.

Dependency management plays a key role in maintaining security. This includes regular updates of dependencies and security patch management. For production systems, vulnerability scanning and monitoring become essential. The implementation should balance staying current with maintaining stability.

Logging and audit trails must be implemented with security in mind. This includes capturing security relevant events while protecting sensitive information. For compliance requirements, maintaining proper audit history becomes crucial. The implementation should support security analysis while managing storage requirements.

Error handling must be implemented securely to prevent information leakage. This includes sanitizing error messages and preventing stack trace exposure. For production systems, maintaining security during error scenarios becomes important. The implementation should provide appropriate feedback while protecting system details.

Access control requires careful implementation at multiple levels. This includes both coarse grained and fine grained permissions management. For real time features, controlling access to specific channels or topics becomes important. The implementation should support complex permission scenarios while maintaining performance.

Database security requires particular attention in real time applications. This includes proper query parameterization and prevention of injection attacks. For distributed systems, maintaining consistent security across database instances becomes crucial. The implementation should prevent unauthorized access while maintaining performance.

Memory management must account for security implications. This includes preventing memory leaks that could lead to denial of service conditions. For long running connections, proper cleanup of sensitive data becomes essential. The implementation should maintain security boundaries while managing resources efficiently.

Network security requires implementation at multiple layers. This includes proper firewall configuration and network segregation. For distributed systems, securing inter node communication becomes particularly important. The implementation should prevent unauthorized network access while maintaining system functionality.

Security monitoring must provide comprehensive visibility. This includes intrusion detection and anomaly monitoring capabilities. For production systems, real time security alerting becomes crucial. The implementation should enable quick response to security incidents while managing false positives.

Backup and recovery procedures must maintain security requirements. This includes proper encryption of backup data and secure storage locations. For disaster recovery scenarios, maintaining security during restoration becomes important. The implementation should prevent unauthorized access to backup data while enabling legitimate recovery.

Security testing should be comprehensive and ongoing. This includes both automated scanning and manual penetration testing. For real time features, testing specific WebSocket attack vectors becomes important. Regular security assessments help maintain system security posture.

Documentation of security procedures supports consistent implementation. This includes security configuration guides and incident response procedures. For team environments, maintaining security awareness becomes crucial. Regular review and updates ensure continued effectiveness of security measures.

Compliance requirements must be properly addressed in security implementation. This includes meeting specific industry standards and regulatory requirements. For international systems, handling varying jurisdictional requirements becomes important. The implementation should maintain compliance while enabling system functionality.

# 55. WebSocket Security

WebSocket security presents unique challenges that require specific attention beyond traditional web application security measures. Real time applications using WebSockets must implement robust security controls while maintaining the performance benefits that make WebSockets valuable.

WebSocket connection security begins with the initial handshake. This crucial phase requires careful implementation of security controls including proper origin validation. The server must verify that connection attempts come from authorized sources and implement appropriate authentication mechanisms. While the WebSocket protocol provides some built in security features, additional application level controls are typically necessary.

Message integrity becomes particularly important in WebSocket applications. Unlike traditional HTTP requests, WebSocket connections maintain a persistent connection where multiple messages may be exchanged. Each message must be validated for both structure and content. Implementing message signatures or other integrity checks helps prevent message tampering during transmission.

Transport Layer Security (TLS) should be mandatory for all WebSocket connections in production environments. The wss:// protocol ensures encryption of all data transmitted between client and server. Certificate management becomes crucial, including proper certificate validation and handling of certificate expiration. Regular rotation of certificates following security best practices helps maintain strong transport security.

Connection authentication requires ongoing validation throughout the WebSocket lifecycle. While initial authentication occurs during handshake, maintaining session validity becomes important for long lived connections. Implementing periodic reauthentication or token refresh mechanisms helps prevent unauthorized access through compromised connections.

Message validation must account for various attack vectors specific to WebSocket communications. This includes protection against oversized messages that could cause memory issues, malformed frames that might exploit protocol implementations, and carefully structured payloads designed to trigger application vulnerabilities. Implementing appropriate message size limits and strict message format validation helps prevent these attacks.

Rate limiting becomes particularly important for WebSocket connections due to their persistent nature. Unlike HTTP requests where each interaction incurs connection overhead, WebSocket connections can rapidly send messages once established. Implementing both connection level and message level rate limiting helps prevent abuse while maintaining service for legitimate users.

Session management for WebSocket connections requires careful consideration. This includes handling session expiration, managing concurrent connections from the same user, and properly cleaning up resources when connections terminate. Implementing appropriate session tracking and cleanup mechanisms helps prevent resource exhaustion and unauthorized access.

Cross Origin Resource Sharing (CORS) policies must be carefully implemented for WebSocket connections. While the same origin policy provides some protection, many applications require connections from different origins. Implementing proper CORS controls helps prevent unauthorized cross origin connections while enabling legitimate integrations.

Protocol level security requires attention to WebSocket specific vulnerabilities. This includes proper handling of control frames, managing fragmentation, and implementing appropriate timeouts. Understanding and properly implementing the WebSocket protocol specification helps prevent protocol level attacks.

Authorization for WebSocket operations must account for real time nature of communications. This includes implementing appropriate channel or topic level access controls and managing permission changes in real time. Proper authorization helps prevent unauthorized access to sensitive data or operations while maintaining application functionality.

Monitoring WebSocket connections requires specific security focused metrics. This includes tracking connection patterns, message rates, and error conditions that might indicate security issues. Implementing appropriate monitoring helps detect and respond to security incidents while maintaining system performance.

Resource management becomes particularly important for security of WebSocket applications. This includes managing memory usage, connection counts, and system resources used by persistent connections. Implementing appropriate resource limits helps prevent denial of service conditions while maintaining service quality.

Error handling for WebSocket connections must maintain security while providing appropriate feedback. This includes properly handling protocol errors, application errors, and security violations. Implementing secure error handling helps prevent information disclosure while maintaining application functionality.

Load balancing of WebSocket connections requires security aware implementation. This includes maintaining session affinity while preventing session fixation, managing SSL termination, and ensuring consistent security controls across multiple servers. Proper load balancer configuration helps maintain security in distributed environments.

Logging of WebSocket security events requires careful implementation. This includes capturing relevant security information while protecting sensitive data and managing log storage requirements. Implementing appropriate logging helps support security analysis and incident response while maintaining compliance requirements.

Testing WebSocket security requires specific tooling and methodologies. This includes testing protocol level security, application level controls, and performance under security related scenarios. Regular security testing helps maintain strong security posture while identifying potential vulnerabilities.

Documentation of WebSocket security controls supports consistent implementation and operation. This includes documenting security configurations, operational procedures, and incident response plans. Maintaining current documentation helps ensure effective security measures across the application lifecycle.

Compliance requirements for WebSocket applications may include specific controls or monitoring capabilities. This includes implementing required security measures and maintaining appropriate audit trails. Understanding and implementing compliance requirements helps maintain regulatory compliance while enabling application functionality.

Regular security review of WebSocket implementations helps maintain strong security posture. This includes reviewing configurations, updating security controls, and adapting to new threats. Ongoing security maintenance helps prevent security degradation while supporting application evolution.

# 56. Rate Limiting in Production

Rate limiting in production environments requires careful consideration and implementation to ensure system stability while maintaining service quality for legitimate users. Production systems face unique challenges that development environments may not encounter, making proper rate limiting crucial for sustained operation.

Implementing rate limiting at scale requires a distributed approach. While single server rate limiting can be relatively straightforward, production environments typically involve multiple servers handling WebSocket connections. This distributed nature necessitates coordination between servers to maintain consistent rate limits across the system.

Redis often serves as an excellent tool for distributed rate limiting. Its atomic operations and built in expiration functionality make it well suited for tracking request rates across multiple servers. Implementing a sliding window rate limiter using Redis allows for precise control while maintaining high performance. The sliding window approach provides more accurate rate limiting compared to fixed window implementations, especially around window boundaries.

Different types of operations may require varying rate limits. Connection establishment might have stricter limits than message transmission once connected. User specific actions could have different limits than system wide operations. Implementing a flexible rate limiting system that can handle these varying requirements helps maintain system stability while providing appropriate service levels.

Burst handling becomes particularly important in production environments. While average request rates might be within limits, sudden bursts of activity can impact system stability. Implementing token bucket algorithms allows for controlled burst handling while maintaining overall rate limits. This approach provides better user experience compared to strict rate limiting while still protecting system resources.

Monitoring rate limiting effectiveness requires specific metrics. This includes tracking limit violations, near limit conditions, and impact on system resources. Implementing appropriate monitoring helps identify potential issues before they impact service quality. Regular review of rate limiting metrics helps tune limits for optimal system performance.

Production rate limiting must account for different client types. Mobile clients might require different limits than web browsers. API clients could have separate limits from interactive users. Implementing client aware rate limiting helps provide appropriate service levels while preventing abuse from any particular client type.

Error handling for rate limited requests requires careful consideration. Providing appropriate feedback helps clients adjust their behavior while maintaining service quality. Implementing retry after headers and clear error messages helps clients handle rate limiting gracefully. This becomes particularly important for automated clients that need to adjust their request patterns.

Geographic distribution of users can impact rate limiting strategies. Different regions might require different limits based on usage patterns or regulatory requirements. Implementing location aware rate limiting helps provide appropriate service levels while maintaining compliance with regional requirements.

Resource consumption must factor into rate limiting decisions. Different operations might consume varying amounts of system resources. Implementing resource aware rate limiting helps prevent system overload while allowing maximum utilization of available capacity. This becomes particularly important for operations that involve significant processing or storage requirements.

Rate limiting configuration needs to be easily adjustable in production. Business requirements or system capacity might necessitate limit changes. Implementing configurable rate limiting allows for dynamic adjustment without service interruption. This flexibility helps maintain service quality while adapting to changing requirements.

Testing rate limiting effectiveness requires specific approaches. Load testing must verify rate limiting behavior under various conditions. Implementing comprehensive testing helps ensure rate limiting performs as expected in production scenarios. This includes testing burst handling, distributed coordination, and error handling behaviors.

Documentation of rate limiting implementation supports effective operation. This includes documenting limit configurations, monitoring approaches, and adjustment procedures. Maintaining current documentation helps ensure consistent operation across the organization. This becomes particularly important during incident response or system modifications.

Compliance requirements might impact rate limiting implementation. Some regulations require specific handling of rate limited requests. Implementing compliant rate limiting helps maintain regulatory compliance while providing appropriate service levels. This includes maintaining required audit trails and implementing mandated handling procedures.

Integration with other system components requires careful consideration. Rate limiting must work effectively with load balancers, caching systems, and application servers. Implementing coordinated rate limiting helps maintain system stability while providing consistent service levels. This coordination becomes particularly important in distributed environments.

Performance impact of rate limiting must be minimized. Implementation overhead should not significantly impact system response times. Efficient rate limiting implementation helps maintain service quality while providing necessary protection. This includes optimizing storage access and minimizing inter server communication.

Regular review of rate limiting effectiveness helps maintain optimal configuration. This includes analyzing usage patterns, system impact, and business requirements. Implementing periodic reviews helps ensure rate limiting continues to meet system needs while maintaining service quality.

Rate limiting strategies must evolve with system changes. New features or architectural changes might require adjusted limits. Implementing adaptable rate limiting helps maintain protection as systems evolve. This flexibility supports continuous system improvement while maintaining stability.

The future of rate limiting involves increasing sophistication. Machine learning might help identify optimal limits and adjust them automatically. Implementing forward looking rate limiting strategies helps prepare for evolving requirements while maintaining current functionality.

# 57. Handling High Concurrency

Handling high concurrency in Elixir and Phoenix applications requires careful consideration of system architecture, resource utilization, and performance optimization. The BEAM virtual machine provides excellent tools for managing concurrent operations, but developers must understand how to leverage these capabilities effectively.

At its core, Elixir's concurrency model is built on the actor pattern, where processes communicate through message passing. This fundamental approach allows applications to scale horizontally across multiple cores and machines. When dealing with high concurrency in production systems, it's crucial to understand how these processes interact and manage their resources.

Process pools become essential when handling large numbers of concurrent connections. While Elixir processes are lightweight, creating appropriate pooling strategies helps manage resource utilization effectively. Tools like poolboy or NimblePool provide robust solutions for managing process pools, ensuring that system resources are used efficiently while maintaining responsiveness.

Connection management plays a crucial role in handling high concurrency. Each WebSocket connection maintains its own process, but careful consideration must be given to connection lifecycle management. Implementing appropriate connection monitoring and cleanup ensures that resources are released promptly when connections terminate, preventing resource leaks that could impact system performance.

State management becomes more complex under high concurrency. While GenServers provide excellent tools for managing state, they can become bottlenecks if not used appropriately. Implementing distributed state management using tools like Phoenix PubSub or implementing CRDT-based solutions helps maintain system responsiveness under high load.

Message queuing strategies become crucial when dealing with high message volumes. While the BEAM handles message queues efficiently, implementing appropriate backpressure mechanisms helps prevent individual processes from becoming overwhelmed. This might involve implementing rate limiting at the process level or using external message queues for specific operations.

Memory management requires special attention under high concurrency. While Elixir's garbage collection operates per process, high numbers of concurrent processes can still impact system memory usage. Implementing appropriate monitoring and optimization strategies helps maintain stable memory utilization even under heavy load.

Process supervision strategies must be carefully considered when handling high concurrency. While the supervisor tree provides excellent fault tolerance, inappropriate restart strategies can cascade into system-wide issues under high load. Implementing appropriate supervision strategies helps maintain system stability while providing necessary fault tolerance.

Load balancing becomes crucial when dealing with high numbers of concurrent connections. While Phoenix channels handle distribution across nodes effectively, implementing appropriate load balancing strategies helps maintain even resource utilization across the cluster. This might involve custom distribution strategies or integration with external load balancers.

Database access patterns require careful optimization under high concurrency. Connection pools must be properly sized, and query patterns must be optimized to prevent database bottlenecks. Implementing appropriate caching strategies and query optimization helps maintain database performance under high concurrent load.

Task management becomes particularly important when handling concurrent operations. While Tasks provide excellent tools for concurrent operation, inappropriate task management can lead to resource exhaustion. Implementing proper task supervision and limiting concurrent task execution helps maintain system stability.

Monitoring becomes crucial under high concurrency. Traditional monitoring approaches might not provide sufficient visibility into system behavior under high load. Implementing appropriate metrics collection and analysis helps identify potential issues before they impact system performance.

Error handling strategies must account for concurrent operation. While individual process failures are isolated, inappropriate error handling can still impact system stability under high load. Implementing robust error handling and recovery strategies helps maintain system reliability while providing appropriate feedback to clients.

Resource limits must be carefully considered when handling high concurrency. While Elixir processes are lightweight, system resources still have limits. Implementing appropriate resource monitoring and limiting helps prevent system overload while maintaining service quality for active connections.

Performance optimization becomes increasingly important under high concurrency. Small inefficiencies can compound significantly when multiplied across many concurrent operations. Regular profiling and optimization helps maintain system performance while handling high concurrent loads effectively.

Network optimization plays a crucial role in handling high concurrency. While WebSocket connections are relatively lightweight, network resource utilization can still impact system performance. Implementing appropriate network optimization strategies helps maintain connection quality under high load.

Testing under high concurrency requires specific approaches. Traditional testing methods might not adequately verify system behavior under concurrent load. Implementing appropriate load testing and verification strategies helps ensure system reliability under high concurrent operation.

Documentation becomes particularly important when dealing with high concurrency. System behavior under load must be well understood by operations teams. Maintaining comprehensive documentation helps ensure effective system operation and incident response under high concurrent load.

Future considerations must account for increasing concurrency requirements. System design should allow for scaling beyond current needs. Implementing forward looking architecture helps ensure systems can handle growing concurrent load while maintaining performance and reliability.

# 58. Database Scaling Strategies

Database scaling strategies in real-time Phoenix applications require careful consideration of both architectural design and operational implementation. As applications grow and handle increasing loads, the database layer often becomes a critical bottleneck that must be addressed through various scaling approaches.

Vertical scaling represents the simplest approach to database scaling, involving the addition of more resources to existing database servers. While this approach can be effective initially, it eventually reaches practical and economic limits. When implementing vertical scaling in Phoenix applications, careful attention must be paid to connection pool configurations and query optimization to maximize the benefits of additional resources.

Horizontal scaling through database sharding becomes necessary for many high-scale applications. In Phoenix applications, implementing sharding requires careful consideration of data access patterns and partition keys. Custom Ecto repos can be implemented to handle sharding logic, directing queries to appropriate database shards based on application-specific criteria. This approach requires careful management of cross-shard queries and transactions.

Read replicas provide another powerful scaling strategy for read-heavy applications. Phoenix applications can be configured to direct read queries to replicas while maintaining write operations on the primary database. This requires careful implementation of replica lag handling and potential eventual consistency concerns, particularly in real-time applications where data freshness expectations may be high.

Connection pooling strategies become crucial as database scaling increases. Tools like DBConnection provide robust pooling capabilities, but proper configuration becomes essential. Pool sizes must be carefully tuned based on application requirements, available database resources, and expected concurrent operation patterns. Monitoring and adjusting these configurations based on production metrics helps maintain optimal performance.

Query optimization takes on increased importance in scaled database environments. Explain plans must be regularly analyzed, and queries must be optimized for distributed execution when applicable. Implementing appropriate indexing strategies becomes crucial, with careful consideration given to index maintenance overhead in write-heavy scenarios.

Caching strategies play a vital role in database scaling. While Phoenix provides excellent caching capabilities through ETS and external caching systems, implementing appropriate cache invalidation strategies becomes crucial in distributed environments. Cache coherency must be maintained across application nodes while preventing excessive database load from cache misses.

Partitioning strategies must be carefully considered when scaling databases. While traditional database partitioning can improve performance, it requires careful planning to maintain query efficiency and data locality. Implementing appropriate partitioning schemes based on application access patterns helps maximize the benefits while minimizing operational complexity.

Write scaling presents particular challenges in real-time applications. While read scaling can often be achieved through replication, write scaling typically requires more complex solutions. Implementing appropriate write batching and queueing strategies helps manage write loads while maintaining system responsiveness.

Monitoring becomes increasingly important in scaled database environments. Traditional monitoring approaches may not provide sufficient visibility into distributed database operations. Implementing comprehensive monitoring across database instances helps identify performance issues and capacity constraints before they impact application performance.

Migration strategies must account for database scaling requirements. While Phoenix provides excellent migration tools, executing migrations across sharded or heavily replicated databases requires careful planning. Implementing appropriate migration strategies helps maintain data consistency while minimizing application impact during schema changes.

Backup and recovery strategies become more complex in scaled database environments. While individual database backups may be straightforward, maintaining consistent backups across distributed databases requires careful coordination. Implementing appropriate backup strategies helps ensure data can be recovered effectively when needed.

Performance optimization in scaled database environments requires ongoing attention. Query patterns that perform well on single databases may need revision when operating across distributed systems. Regular performance analysis and optimization helps maintain system responsiveness as scale increases.

Data consistency requirements must be carefully considered when implementing database scaling. While strong consistency might be necessary for certain operations, relaxing consistency requirements where appropriate can significantly improve scalability. Implementing appropriate consistency models based on application requirements helps balance performance and data integrity.

Transaction management becomes more complex in distributed database environments. While Phoenix and Ecto provide excellent transaction support, distributed transactions require careful handling to maintain performance and reliability. Implementing appropriate transaction strategies helps maintain data integrity while minimizing performance impact.

Security considerations take on additional complexity in scaled database environments. While individual database security might be straightforward, maintaining consistent security across distributed databases requires careful planning. Implementing appropriate security controls helps protect data while maintaining system accessibility.

Operational procedures must account for database scaling strategies. While routine maintenance might be straightforward on single databases, coordinating operations across distributed databases requires careful planning. Implementing appropriate operational procedures helps maintain system reliability while minimizing maintenance impact.

Future growth considerations must be incorporated into database scaling strategies. While current scaling approaches might meet immediate needs, planning for future growth helps ensure systems can evolve effectively. Implementing forward-looking scaling strategies helps maintain system performance and reliability as requirements grow.

Cost management becomes increasingly important as database scaling increases. While scaling can improve performance, it often comes with significant cost implications. Implementing appropriate cost monitoring and optimization helps maintain system efficiency while managing operational expenses effectively.

Documentation becomes crucial for scaled database environments. While single database operations might be well understood, distributed database operations often require more detailed documentation. Maintaining comprehensive documentation helps ensure effective system operation and incident response in scaled environments.

# 59. Caching in Production

Caching in production environments for Phoenix applications requires a strategic and layered approach to effectively support real-time features while maintaining performance under load. Production caching introduces complexities that development environments often don't encounter, necessitating careful consideration of cache invalidation, consistency, and resource utilization.

Distributed caching becomes essential in production environments where multiple application nodes operate concurrently. While Phoenix applications can leverage ETS for local caching, production deployments often require distributed caching solutions like Redis or Memcached. These systems provide consistent caching across all application nodes while offering features like automatic failover and replication.

Cache warming strategies play a crucial role in production environments. Cold caches can lead to performance degradation during application startup or after deployments. Implementing appropriate cache warming procedures helps maintain system performance during transitions. This might involve pre-populating caches with frequently accessed data or implementing progressive cache warming based on access patterns.

Cache invalidation strategies become more complex in production environments where multiple data sources and application nodes are involved. While simple time-based expiration might suffice for some scenarios, production applications often require more sophisticated invalidation approaches. Event-based cache invalidation, where changes to underlying data trigger cache updates, helps maintain cache consistency while minimizing unnecessary invalidations.

Memory management takes on increased importance when implementing production caching. While development environments might have ample memory resources, production caches must be carefully sized to prevent memory exhaustion. Implementing appropriate cache eviction policies helps maintain system stability while maximizing cache effectiveness.

Cache hit rates must be carefully monitored in production environments. While development environments might not focus on cache performance metrics, production systems require comprehensive monitoring of cache effectiveness. Implementing appropriate monitoring helps identify opportunities for cache optimization and potential issues before they impact system performance.

Fault tolerance becomes crucial for production caching systems. While cache failures in development might be easily handled, production environments require robust failure handling mechanisms. Implementing appropriate fallback strategies helps maintain system operation even when caching systems experience issues.

Security considerations take on additional importance for production caches. While development environments might not focus on cache security, production systems must protect cached data from unauthorized access. Implementing appropriate access controls and encryption helps maintain data security while preserving cache performance.

Cache coherency must be maintained across distributed systems in production environments. While single-node applications might not encounter coherency issues, distributed systems require careful management of cache updates. Implementing appropriate coherency protocols helps prevent inconsistencies while maintaining system performance.

Performance optimization for production caches requires ongoing attention. While development environments might not focus on cache performance tuning, production systems require regular optimization to maintain effectiveness. Implementing appropriate performance monitoring and optimization helps maximize cache benefits while minimizing resource utilization.

Network considerations become crucial for distributed caching in production. While development environments might operate on local networks, production systems often span multiple data centers or cloud regions. Implementing appropriate network optimization helps maintain cache performance while minimizing latency impact.

Cost management for production caching requires careful consideration. While development environments might not focus on operational costs, production caching can significantly impact infrastructure expenses. Implementing appropriate cost monitoring and optimization helps maintain system efficiency while managing operational costs effectively.

Cache persistence strategies become important in production environments. While development caches might be ephemeral, production systems often require persistent caching to maintain performance across system restarts. Implementing appropriate persistence mechanisms helps maintain cache effectiveness while ensuring data durability when needed.

Monitoring and alerting systems must account for cache performance in production. While development environments might not require comprehensive monitoring, production systems need detailed visibility into cache operation. Implementing appropriate monitoring helps identify issues quickly while maintaining system reliability.

Operational procedures must account for cache management in production. While development environments might not require formal procedures, production systems need clear processes for cache maintenance and troubleshooting. Implementing appropriate operational procedures helps maintain system reliability while minimizing maintenance impact.

Version management becomes crucial when deploying cache changes to production. While development environments might handle cache changes casually, production deployments require careful coordination of cache updates. Implementing appropriate version management helps maintain system stability during deployments.

Documentation becomes essential for production caching systems. While development environments might rely on tribal knowledge, production systems require comprehensive documentation of caching strategies and procedures. Maintaining detailed documentation helps ensure effective system operation and incident response.

Backup strategies must account for cache data in production environments. While development caches might be disposable, production systems often require backup mechanisms for critical cached data. Implementing appropriate backup strategies helps ensure data can be recovered effectively when needed.

Resource allocation for production caches requires careful planning. While development environments might have flexible resources, production systems need precise allocation of cache resources. Implementing appropriate resource management helps maintain system performance while optimizing infrastructure utilization.

Future scalability must be considered when implementing production caching. While current caching approaches might meet immediate needs, planning for future growth helps ensure systems can evolve effectively. Implementing forward-looking caching strategies helps maintain system performance and reliability as requirements grow.

# 60. Performance Tuning

Performance tuning in real time Phoenix applications requires a systematic and data driven approach to identify and resolve bottlenecks while maintaining system reliability. The process involves careful analysis of multiple system components and their interactions to optimize overall application performance.

Application performance profiling serves as the foundation for effective tuning. While basic performance metrics provide useful insights, comprehensive profiling helps identify specific areas requiring optimization. Tools like :observer and erlang:trace() enable detailed analysis of system behavior under various conditions. This information guides optimization efforts by highlighting actual bottlenecks rather than perceived issues.

Memory utilization often presents significant optimization opportunities in Phoenix applications. The Erlang VM's garbage collection behavior can impact application responsiveness, particularly during peak loads. Tuning garbage collection parameters and implementing appropriate memory management strategies helps maintain consistent performance. This might involve adjusting generation settings or implementing custom memory management approaches for specific use cases.

Process management plays a crucial role in Phoenix application performance. While the Erlang VM excels at managing large numbers of processes, inappropriate process usage patterns can impact system performance. Analyzing process behavior and implementing appropriate pooling strategies helps optimize resource utilization while maintaining system responsiveness.

Database interaction typically offers substantial performance optimization potential. While basic database queries might perform adequately, production workloads often require careful query optimization. Implementing appropriate indexing strategies, query optimization, and connection pooling helps maintain database performance under load. Regular analysis of database access patterns helps identify optimization opportunities.

WebSocket connection handling presents unique performance considerations. While Phoenix channels provide efficient WebSocket support, optimizing connection handling helps maintain system performance at scale. This might involve implementing appropriate connection pooling, message batching, or custom socket options based on specific application requirements.

Network optimization becomes crucial for distributed Phoenix applications. While basic network configuration might suffice for simple deployments, production systems often require careful network tuning. Implementing appropriate TCP options, load balancing strategies, and network topology helps optimize communication between system components.

Code optimization provides another avenue for performance improvement. While Elixir code generally performs well, certain patterns can impact system performance. Profiling code execution and implementing appropriate optimizations helps maintain system efficiency. This might involve restructuring algorithms, implementing caching, or leveraging native implementations for performance critical operations.

Message passing patterns significantly impact distributed system performance. While basic message passing works well for simple interactions, optimizing message patterns helps maintain system performance under load. This might involve implementing appropriate batching strategies, message compression, or custom serialization approaches based on specific requirements.

Process supervision strategies affect both system reliability and performance. While basic supervision trees provide fault tolerance, optimizing supervisor configuration helps maintain system performance during failure scenarios. This might involve implementing appropriate restart strategies, process grouping, or custom supervision approaches based on specific requirements.

State management optimization becomes crucial for maintaining system performance. While basic state management approaches work well for simple cases, optimizing state handling helps maintain system efficiency at scale. This might involve implementing appropriate state partitioning, replication strategies, or custom state management approaches based on specific requirements.

Resource pooling strategies significantly impact system performance. While basic pooling mechanisms provide resource management, optimizing pool configuration helps maintain system efficiency under varying loads. This might involve implementing adaptive pooling strategies, custom resource management, or specialized pooling approaches based on specific requirements.

Event handling optimization affects real time feature performance. While basic event handling works well for simple cases, optimizing event processing helps maintain system responsiveness under load. This might involve implementing appropriate event batching, prioritization strategies, or custom event handling approaches based on specific requirements.

Cache utilization patterns significantly impact system performance. While basic caching provides performance benefits, optimizing cache usage helps maximize system efficiency. This might involve implementing appropriate cache warming strategies, invalidation approaches, or custom caching mechanisms based on specific requirements.

Concurrency management optimization becomes crucial at scale. While Elixir handles concurrency well, optimizing concurrent operations helps maintain system performance under load. This might involve implementing appropriate concurrency limits, backpressure mechanisms, or custom concurrent processing approaches based on specific requirements.

Load testing plays a vital role in performance tuning. While basic testing provides useful insights, comprehensive load testing helps identify performance bottlenecks under realistic conditions. Implementing appropriate load testing scenarios helps validate optimization efforts while ensuring system reliability.

Monitoring integration enables ongoing performance optimization. While basic monitoring provides useful metrics, comprehensive monitoring helps identify performance trends and potential issues. Implementing appropriate monitoring strategies helps maintain system performance while enabling proactive optimization.

Documentation becomes essential for maintaining optimization efforts. While basic documentation provides useful reference material, comprehensive documentation helps ensure optimization knowledge is preserved and shared effectively. Maintaining detailed documentation of performance tuning decisions and outcomes helps guide future optimization efforts.

Regular review and adjustment of performance tuning measures ensures continued effectiveness. While initial optimization provides performance improvements, ongoing analysis helps identify new optimization opportunities as system requirements evolve. Implementing appropriate review processes helps maintain system performance over time.

The iterative nature of performance tuning requires patience and methodical analysis. While quick fixes might provide temporary relief, sustainable performance improvement requires systematic optimization based on actual system behavior and requirements.

# 61. Troubleshooting Common Issues

Troubleshooting real time Phoenix applications requires a systematic approach and deep understanding of common issues that can arise in production environments. When problems occur, having a structured methodology for identifying and resolving issues helps minimize downtime and maintain system reliability.

Connection handling issues frequently arise in real time applications. Users may experience intermittent disconnections, delayed message delivery, or complete connection failures. These problems often stem from network configuration issues, improper connection handling, or resource constraints. Investigating connection logs, monitoring network metrics, and analyzing client behavior helps identify the root cause. Common solutions include adjusting keepalive settings, implementing proper connection cleanup, and optimizing connection pooling configurations.

State synchronization problems can manifest in various ways across distributed systems. Users might see inconsistent data, stale information, or conflicting updates. These issues typically result from race conditions, improper state management, or network partitions. Debugging requires careful analysis of state propagation patterns, event ordering, and conflict resolution mechanisms. Solutions often involve implementing proper consistency protocols, improving state replication strategies, and enhancing conflict detection mechanisms.

Performance degradation represents another common category of issues. Applications might experience increased latency, reduced throughput, or resource exhaustion. These problems frequently stem from inefficient resource utilization, unoptimized queries, or scaling limitations. Investigation requires comprehensive performance profiling, resource monitoring, and load analysis. Resolution typically involves optimizing critical paths, implementing caching strategies, and adjusting resource allocation.

Memory management issues can significantly impact application stability. Systems might experience memory leaks, excessive garbage collection, or out of memory errors. These problems often result from improper resource cleanup, accumulated state, or inefficient data structures. Debugging requires memory profiling, leak detection, and garbage collection analysis. Solutions typically involve implementing proper cleanup mechanisms, optimizing data structures, and adjusting memory management parameters.

Process management problems can affect system reliability. Applications might experience process crashes, supervision failures, or deadlocks. These issues commonly stem from improper error handling, flawed supervision strategies, or resource contention. Investigation requires process monitoring, crash analysis, and supervision tree inspection. Resolution often involves improving error handling, adjusting supervision strategies, and optimizing process interactions.

Database interaction issues can disrupt application functionality. Users might experience query timeouts, connection failures, or data inconsistencies. These problems typically result from connection pool exhaustion, unoptimized queries, or concurrent acccss patterns. Debugging requires query analysis, connection monitoring, and transaction inspection. Solutions often involve optimizing queries, adjusting pool configurations, and implementing proper concurrency controls.

Message routing problems can affect real time feature reliability. Systems might experience message loss, ordering issues, or delivery delays. These issues commonly stem from improper routing configuration, network problems, or capacity limitations. Investigation requires message flow analysis, routing inspection, and delivery monitoring. Resolution typically involves optimizing routing strategies, improving network configuration, and enhancing message handling.

Authentication and authorization issues can compromise system security. Users might experience access problems, token failures, or permission inconsistencies. These problems often result from improper token handling, misconfigured permissions, or session management issues. Debugging requires authentication flow analysis, permission verification, and session monitoring. Solutions typically involve improving token management, enhancing permission controls, and optimizing session handling.

Scaling related issues can emerge as system load increases. Applications might experience resource contention, coordination problems, or performance bottlenecks. These issues commonly stem from architectural limitations, resource constraints, or coordination overhead. Investigation requires scalability analysis, resource monitoring, and bottleneck identification. Resolution often involves architectural improvements, resource optimization, and enhanced coordination mechanisms.

Integration related problems can affect system functionality. Applications might experience API failures, service unavailability, or data synchronization issues. These problems typically result from service dependencies, integration patterns, or network connectivity. Debugging requires integration flow analysis, service monitoring, and dependency inspection. Solutions often involve improving integration patterns, enhancing error handling, and optimizing service interactions.

Monitoring and logging issues can hinder problem resolution. Systems might experience insufficient visibility, missing information, or monitoring overhead. These problems commonly stem from inadequate instrumentation, improper log levels, or resource constraints. Investigation requires monitoring analysis, log inspection, and instrumentation review. Resolution typically involves enhancing instrumentation, optimizing log levels, and improving monitoring efficiency.

Recovery mechanism failures can impact system reliability. Applications might experience improper failover, incomplete recovery, or state inconsistencies. These issues often result from flawed recovery procedures, state management problems, or coordination failures. Debugging requires recovery flow analysis, state verification, and failure scenario testing. Solutions typically involve improving recovery procedures, enhancing state management, and optimizing coordination mechanisms.

Configuration related issues can cause system problems. Users might experience unexpected behavior, feature unavailability, or performance issues. These problems commonly stem from misconfiguration, environment differences, or deployment issues. Investigation requires configuration analysis, environment comparison, and deployment verification. Resolution often involves improving configuration management, enhancing deployment procedures, and optimizing environment handling.

Regular review and documentation of troubleshooting experiences helps build organizational knowledge and improves future problem resolution efficiency. Maintaining detailed records of issues, their root causes, and resolution approaches provides valuable reference material for similar problems. This documentation should include specific symptoms, investigation steps, and implemented solutions to facilitate faster problem resolution in the future.

# 62. Maintenance and Updates

Maintaining and updating real time Phoenix applications requires careful planning and execution to ensure system stability while introducing new features and improvements. A well structured maintenance strategy helps prevent issues and enables smooth updates across distributed systems.

Regular dependency updates form a critical part of application maintenance. Phoenix applications typically rely on numerous dependencies, including the Phoenix framework itself, Elixir libraries, and various other packages. Keeping these dependencies current helps ensure security, performance, and compatibility. However, updating dependencies requires thorough testing to verify that existing functionality remains intact. Creating comprehensive test suites that cover real time features, WebSocket interactions, and distributed system behavior helps validate updates before deployment.

Database maintenance plays a vital role in system health. Regular optimization of database queries, index maintenance, and schema updates help maintain performance as data volumes grow. Implementing database migrations requires careful consideration of real time features to prevent disruption of active connections and ongoing operations. Planning maintenance windows and implementing rolling updates helps minimize impact on users while ensuring database health.

Application code maintenance involves regular refactoring, optimization, and technical debt management. As real time features evolve, code patterns may need adjustment to maintain performance and reliability. Implementing new patterns or improving existing implementations requires careful consideration of backward compatibility and state management. Documentation maintenance ensures that development teams can effectively maintain and extend the system.

Infrastructure maintenance encompasses server updates, network configuration changes, and monitoring system updates. Regular security patches and system updates help maintain infrastructure health. Planning maintenance windows for infrastructure updates requires coordination across distributed systems to maintain availability. Implementing redundancy and failover mechanisms helps minimize impact during maintenance operations.

Monitoring system maintenance ensures continued visibility into application health and performance. Regular updates to monitoring tools, alert configurations, and dashboards help maintain effective system oversight. Reviewing and adjusting monitoring thresholds based on system growth and behavior patterns helps maintain accurate alerting. Maintaining historical monitoring data aids in capacity planning and trend analysis.

Configuration management requires regular review and updates to maintain system effectiveness. As applications scale and evolve, configuration parameters may need adjustment to optimize performance and resource utilization. Maintaining configuration version control and documentation helps track changes and understand their impact. Implementing configuration validation helps prevent issues from misconfiguration.

Performance optimization represents an ongoing maintenance requirement. Regular performance reviews help identify opportunities for improvement and potential issues before they impact users. Maintaining performance test suites and benchmarks helps validate optimization efforts. Implementing performance monitoring and alerting helps maintain awareness of system behavior.

Security maintenance involves regular security audits, vulnerability assessments, and penetration testing. Keeping security configurations current and implementing security patches helps protect system integrity. Maintaining security documentation and incident response procedures helps ensure effective security management. Regular security training helps maintain team awareness and capabilities.

Backup and recovery system maintenance ensures continued data protection and system resilience. Regular backup verification and recovery testing helps maintain confidence in system recovery capabilities. Maintaining backup retention policies and implementing automated verification helps ensure data availability. Documenting recovery procedures helps maintain operational readiness.

Documentation maintenance supports ongoing system operation and evolution. Keeping technical documentation, operational procedures, and architectural documentation current helps maintain system knowledge. Maintaining troubleshooting guides and known issue documentation helps support operational teams. Regular documentation review helps identify areas needing updates or clarification.

Team knowledge maintenance helps ensure continued system support capabilities. Regular knowledge sharing sessions, training updates, and skill development help maintain team effectiveness. Documenting system knowledge and maintaining operational procedures helps preserve institutional knowledge. Implementing mentoring programs helps develop team capabilities.

Capacity planning represents an ongoing maintenance requirement. Regular review of system resource utilization, growth patterns, and performance metrics helps plan for future needs. Maintaining capacity models and growth projections helps guide infrastructure planning. Implementing capacity monitoring and alerting helps maintain awareness of resource utilization.

Update planning requires careful consideration of system impact and coordination across teams. Planning update sequences, testing requirements, and rollback procedures helps ensure smooth updates. Maintaining update documentation and procedures helps ensure consistent execution. Implementing update verification helps validate successful deployment.

Release management involves coordinating various maintenance activities and updates. Planning release schedules, managing dependencies, and coordinating team activities helps maintain system stability. Maintaining release documentation and procedures helps ensure effective execution. Implementing release validation helps verify successful deployment.

Incident management requires ongoing maintenance to ensure effective response capabilities. Regular review and updates to incident response procedures helps maintain operational effectiveness. Maintaining incident documentation and lessons learned helps improve future responses. Implementing incident review processes helps identify improvement opportunities.

Change management helps control system modifications and maintain stability. Regular review of change procedures and documentation helps ensure effective process execution. Maintaining change logs and impact assessments helps track system evolution. Implementing change verification helps validate modifications.

Through careful attention to these maintenance aspects and regular updates, real time Phoenix applications can maintain reliability, performance, and security while evolving to meet changing requirements. Regular review and adjustment of maintenance procedures helps ensure their continued effectiveness and supports ongoing system health.

# 63. Disaster Recovery

Disaster recovery planning and implementation represents a critical aspect of maintaining reliable real time Phoenix applications. A comprehensive disaster recovery strategy ensures business continuity and data preservation in the face of catastrophic events while minimizing downtime and data loss.

The foundation of effective disaster recovery begins with thorough risk assessment and impact analysis. Organizations must identify potential disaster scenarios ranging from hardware failures and network outages to natural disasters and cyber attacks. Understanding the impact of these scenarios on real time features, WebSocket connections, and distributed system components helps determine appropriate recovery strategies and priorities.

Data backup forms a cornerstone of disaster recovery planning. Real time applications often manage both persistent data in databases and ephemeral state in memory. Implementing regular backups of database content, configuration data, and system state helps ensure recovery capabilities. Distributed systems require particular attention to maintaining consistency across backups from multiple nodes. Automated backup verification and recovery testing helps ensure backup integrity and recovery feasibility.

Recovery point objectives (RPO) and recovery time objectives (RTO) guide disaster recovery planning. Real time applications often require minimal data loss and rapid recovery to maintain user experience and business operations. Determining acceptable RPO and RTO values helps guide technology choices and recovery procedures. Implementing appropriate replication and redundancy mechanisms helps achieve these objectives.

Geographic distribution provides resilience against localized disasters. Implementing multi region deployments with data replication helps maintain availability during regional outages.

Phoenix applications can leverage distributed Erlang capabilities to manage multi region deployments. Careful consideration of data consistency requirements and network latency impacts helps guide geographic distribution strategies.

Failover mechanisms enable rapid recovery from component failures. Implementing automatic failover for critical system components helps minimize downtime. Phoenix applications can leverage OTP supervision trees and distributed Erlang features to manage process failover. Database failover requires particular attention to maintaining data consistency and managing connection pools.

Recovery procedures must address both technical and operational aspects. Detailed documentation of recovery steps, configuration requirements, and verification procedures helps ensure successful execution under pressure. Regular testing of recovery procedures helps identify issues and maintain team familiarity. Implementing automated recovery where possible helps reduce human error and recovery time.

State recovery presents particular challenges for real time applications. WebSocket connections must be reestablished and application state rebuilt after recovery. Implementing graceful connection handling and state reconstruction mechanisms helps manage recovery impact on users. Presence information and real time features may require special handling during recovery.

Communication planning forms an essential part of disaster recovery. Establishing communication procedures and channels helps coordinate recovery efforts and keep stakeholders informed. Implementing status monitoring and notification systems helps maintain awareness of recovery progress. Regular communication testing helps ensure effectiveness during actual disasters.

Team preparation through training and drills helps ensure effective disaster response. Regular review of recovery procedures and hands on practice helps maintain readiness. Implementing incident command structures helps coordinate recovery efforts. Cross training team members helps maintain recovery capabilities despite individual availability.

Infrastructure recovery requires careful sequencing and verification. Establishing component dependencies and startup orders helps ensure proper system initialization. Implementing health checks and verification procedures helps validate recovery progress. Configuration management systems help ensure consistent recovery across environments.

Data consistency verification forms a critical part of recovery procedures. Implementing automated consistency checks helps identify and resolve data issues. Database recovery may require special handling for real time features and distributed state. Maintaining audit trails helps track and verify data recovery.

Security considerations remain important during disaster recovery. Maintaining security controls and access restrictions helps prevent unauthorized access during recovery. Implementing secure communication channels helps protect sensitive data and operations. Security verification helps ensure maintained protection after recovery.

Performance monitoring during recovery helps identify issues and verify system health. Implementing comprehensive monitoring helps track recovery progress and system behavior. Establishing performance baselines helps identify normal operation restoration. Maintaining historical performance data helps verify successful recovery.

Cost management represents an important aspect of disaster recovery planning. Understanding recovery costs and maintaining appropriate resources helps ensure recovery capability. Implementing cost effective redundancy and replication helps balance protection and expense. Regular review of disaster recovery costs helps maintain appropriate investment.

Regular testing and validation helps maintain disaster recovery capabilities. Implementing scheduled recovery tests helps verify procedures and identify issues. Testing should include both technical and operational aspects. Maintaining test documentation helps track capability evolution.

Continuous improvement through review and updates helps maintain recovery effectiveness. Regular assessment of recovery capabilities and requirements helps identify improvement opportunities. Implementing lessons learned from tests and actual recoveries helps enhance procedures. Documentation updates help maintain accuracy and usefulness.

Through comprehensive disaster recovery planning and regular testing, real time Phoenix applications can maintain business continuity and data protection despite catastrophic events. Regular review and updates help ensure continued effectiveness as systems evolve and requirements change.

# 64. Production Checklist

A production checklist serves as a critical tool for ensuring your real time Phoenix application is ready for production deployment and can handle real world demands. This comprehensive guide covers the essential aspects that need verification before going live.

System architecture validation forms the foundation of production readiness. Review your application's overall architecture, ensuring proper separation of concerns and scalability considerations. Verify that your WebSocket connections, Phoenix channels, and LiveView implementations follow best practices for performance and maintainability. Examine your supervision trees and process management strategies to confirm they provide appropriate fault tolerance.

Infrastructure configuration requires thorough verification. Check that your production environment includes appropriate monitoring, logging, and alerting systems. Verify that your deployment tools and procedures are properly configured and tested. Ensure your load balancers, reverse proxies, and other infrastructure components are optimized for WebSocket traffic and long lived connections.

Security measures demand careful review before production deployment. Verify that all sensitive configuration values are properly secured and not exposed in source code or logs. Confirm that your authentication and authorization systems are properly implemented and tested. Review your rate limiting and throttling configurations to protect against abuse. Ensure your SSL/TLS configurations follow current security best practices.

Performance optimization represents a critical checklist area. Verify that your application has undergone thorough load testing and performance profiling. Check that database queries are optimized and appropriate indexes are in place. Confirm that your caching strategies are properly implemented and tested. Review your real time feature implementations for potential performance bottlenecks.

Database management requires specific attention. Verify your database backup procedures are properly configured and tested. Confirm that your database connections are properly pooled and managed. Check that your database scaling strategy is appropriate for your expected load. Review your data retention and archival policies.

State management strategies need careful verification. Review your distributed state handling mechanisms, ensuring proper synchronization across nodes. Verify that your presence tracking implementations can handle expected user loads. Confirm that your real time feature state management follows best practices for consistency and performance.

Error handling deserves thorough examination. Verify that all error conditions are properly caught and handled. Confirm that error messages provide appropriate information without exposing sensitive details. Check that your error reporting systems are properly configured. Review your error recovery procedures for various failure scenarios.

Monitoring systems must be properly configured. Verify that your metrics collection covers all critical system aspects. Confirm that your alerting thresholds are appropriately set. Check that your logging provides sufficient detail for troubleshooting. Review your monitoring dashboards for completeness and usability.

Scaling capabilities require verification. Review your horizontal and vertical scaling strategies. Confirm that your application can handle node additions and removals gracefully. Check that your load balancing configuration properly distributes WebSocket connections. Verify that your database can scale to meet expected demands.

Deployment procedures need careful examination. Verify that your deployment pipeline includes appropriate testing and validation steps. Confirm that your rollback procedures are properly documented and tested. Check that your configuration management handles environment differences correctly. Review your zero downtime deployment capabilities.

Documentation requires comprehensive review. Verify that your operational procedures are properly documented. Confirm that your API documentation is complete and accurate. Check that your troubleshooting guides cover common scenarios. Review your incident response procedures for completeness.

Testing coverage should be verified. Review your test suite coverage across unit, integration, and end to end tests. Confirm that your real time features have appropriate testing. Check that your load testing scenarios reflect expected usage patterns. Verify that your security testing covers potential vulnerabilities.

Resource management needs careful consideration. Review your memory management practices and monitoring. Confirm that your CPU utilization patterns are sustainable. Check that your network capacity can handle expected traffic. Verify that your disk usage patterns and cleanup procedures are appropriate.

Backup and recovery capabilities require verification. Review your backup procedures and schedules. Confirm that your disaster recovery procedures are documented and tested. Check that your data retention policies meet business requirements. Verify that your backup restoration procedures work as expected.

Third party service integration deserves attention. Review your external service dependencies and failure handling. Confirm that your service level agreements meet business needs. Check that your fallback procedures handle service outages appropriately. Verify that your monitoring covers external service health.

By systematically working through this production checklist, you can ensure your real time Phoenix application is ready for production deployment. Regular review and updates to your checklist help maintain production readiness as your application evolves. Remember that production readiness is an ongoing process requiring continuous attention and improvement.

# 65. Future-Proofing Your Application

Future proofing your real time Phoenix application requires careful consideration of both technical and architectural decisions that will impact long term maintainability and scalability. This chapter explores strategies to ensure your application can adapt to changing requirements and technologies while remaining performant and maintainable.

Embracing extensible architectures forms the foundation of future proofing. Design your application with clear boundaries between components, allowing individual pieces to evolve independently. Consider using bounded contexts and well defined interfaces between different parts of your system. This approach makes it easier to replace or upgrade components as requirements change or new technologies emerge.

Version management plays a crucial role in future proofing. Implement proper versioning for your WebSocket protocols, APIs, and data structures. Consider how you'll handle protocol upgrades while maintaining backward compatibility for existing clients. Design your LiveView components and channel implementations to support multiple versions simultaneously during transition periods.

Data storage flexibility ensures your application can adapt to changing requirements. Design your database schemas to be extensible, allowing for new fields and relationships without breaking existing functionality. Consider using schemaless portions for data that may evolve rapidly. Implement data migration strategies that can handle large scale changes without significant downtime.

Scalability planning requires forward thinking. Design your application architecture to handle orders of magnitude more load than current requirements. Consider how your WebSocket connection handling, presence tracking, and real time features will scale. Plan for both vertical and horizontal scaling, ensuring your architecture can take advantage of additional resources when needed.

Technology independence helps protect against obsolescence. Avoid tight coupling to specific technologies or services that may become outdated. Design your interfaces and abstractions to allow for replacement of underlying implementations. Consider how you might migrate to new versions of Phoenix, Elixir, or other dependencies without requiring a complete rewrite.

Performance headroom provides flexibility for future enhancements. Design your system to utilize only a fraction of available resources under normal conditions. This approach allows for adding new features or handling increased load without immediate infrastructure changes. Monitor performance trends to predict when upgrades will be needed.

Code organization impacts long term maintainability. Structure your codebase to support team growth and feature expansion. Consider how new developers will understand and modify the system. Implement clear patterns for adding new real time features, channels, and LiveView components. Document architectural decisions and their rationales.

Testing strategies need to evolve with your application. Design your test suite to be maintainable and extensible. Consider how you'll test new features and integrations. Implement automated testing patterns that can scale with your application's complexity. Plan for testing distributed scenarios and real time feature interactions.

Monitoring and observability require future consideration. Design your monitoring systems to handle increased complexity and scale. Plan how you'll track new metrics and detect emerging patterns. Consider how your logging and tracing capabilities will scale with increased traffic and feature sets.

Security measures must adapt to new threats. Design your authentication and authorization systems to support new requirements and security standards. Consider how you'll implement new security features without disrupting existing functionality. Plan for regular security audits and updates.

Configuration management impacts flexibility. Design your configuration systems to handle new environments and requirements. Consider how you'll manage an increasing number of configuration options. Implement validation and documentation for configuration changes.

Deployment processes need to scale with complexity. Design your deployment pipeline to handle more frequent updates and larger codebases. Consider how you'll maintain zero downtime deployments as your application grows. Plan for managing multiple environments and deployment targets.

Documentation requires ongoing attention. Maintain living documentation that evolves with your application. Consider how you'll document new features and architectural changes. Implement processes for keeping documentation current and accessible.

Error handling strategies must evolve. Design your error handling to accommodate new failure modes and recovery scenarios. Consider how you'll detect and respond to emerging issues. Plan for handling errors in new features and integrations.

Resource management needs future planning. Design your resource allocation and management strategies to handle growth. Consider how you'll manage increasing memory, CPU, and network requirements. Plan for efficient resource utilization at scale.

Integration capabilities require flexibility. Design your integration points to handle new services and protocols. Consider how you'll adapt to changing external requirements. Plan for managing an increasing number of integrations.

Team growth impacts application evolution. Design your development processes to support larger teams and more complex features. Consider how you'll maintain knowledge sharing and code quality. Plan for onboarding new team members efficiently.

By implementing these future proofing strategies, you can build a real time Phoenix application that remains maintainable and adaptable. Regular review of these aspects helps ensure your application can evolve to meet changing requirements while maintaining performance and reliability. Remember that future proofing is an ongoing process requiring continuous evaluation and adjustment of your strategies.

# 66. Real World Case Studies

Building on the theme of future proofing covered in the previous chapter, let's explore real world case studies and practical examples of how organizations have successfully scaled and maintained their real time Phoenix applications.

One particularly instructive example comes from a financial technology company that built their trading platform using Phoenix LiveView and WebSockets. Initially serving a few hundred concurrent users, they needed to scale to support over 100,000 simultaneous connections. Their journey highlights several key architectural decisions that enabled successful scaling.

The team implemented a multi layered caching strategy, combining process based caching using ETS tables for frequently accessed data with a distributed Redis cluster for shared state. This hybrid approach allowed them to maintain sub millisecond response times even as their user base grew. They carefully monitored cache hit rates and adjusted their caching strategies based on actual usage patterns.

Database scaling presented another significant challenge. The team found that their initial approach of using a single PostgreSQL instance couldn't handle the increasing write load from real time trading activities. They implemented a read replica strategy, routing read heavy operations to secondary databases while maintaining a primary database for writes. This separation allowed them to scale their read capacity independently of write capacity.

Connection management proved crucial for handling large numbers of WebSocket connections. The team implemented a custom connection draining system that could gradually migrate users between nodes during deployments. This allowed them to perform zero downtime updates even with thousands of active connections. They also built sophisticated connection monitoring tools to track connection quality and automatically reconnect users experiencing network issues.

Another interesting case study comes from a healthcare monitoring system that needed to process real time data from medical devices. Their architecture evolved to handle increasing numbers of devices and stricter regulatory requirements. They implemented a message queue based system using RabbitMQ to buffer device data, allowing them to handle spikes in incoming data without overwhelming their processing capacity.

The healthcare system's team paid particular attention to data consistency and reliability. They implemented an event sourcing pattern where all device readings were stored as immutable events. This approach allowed them to reconstruct the state of any device at any point in time, which proved invaluable for audit compliance and troubleshooting. They used Phoenix PubSub to distribute processed events to interested subscribers while maintaining strict ordering guarantees.

A social media analytics company provides another valuable example of scaling real time features. They needed to process millions of social media interactions per minute and provide real time analytics to thousands of dashboard users. Their solution involved a combination of stream processing using GenStage and batch processing for historical data. They implemented custom LiveView components that could efficiently render large datasets while maintaining responsive updates.

The analytics team faced particular challenges around memory management. They implemented careful monitoring of LiveView process memory usage and developed strategies for gracefully degrading functionality when under memory pressure. They also built custom garbage collection triggers to help manage memory usage during peak loads.

Authentication and authorization scaling presented unique challenges across these cases. Many teams found that their initial role based access control systems became unwieldy as they added more granular permissions. Solutions often involved implementing attribute based access control systems that could more flexibly handle complex permission rules while maintaining performance.

Monitoring and observability evolved significantly in these systems. Teams frequently started with basic metrics around response times and error rates but needed to expand to include business level metrics and detailed performance tracing. Many implemented distributed tracing using tools like OpenTelemetry to track requests across their distributed systems.

Error handling strategies also matured over time. Teams found that simply logging errors wasn't sufficient at scale. They implemented sophisticated error aggregation and analysis systems to identify patterns and potential issues before they impacted users. Many adopted circuit breaker patterns to gracefully degrade functionality when downstream services experienced issues.

These case studies highlight common patterns in successful scaling strategies. Teams consistently found that investing in monitoring and observability early paid dividends as systems grew more complex. They also discovered that implementing gradual degradation mechanisms helped maintain core functionality during unexpected load spikes or partial system failures.

Performance optimization often focused on reducing unnecessary work rather than just adding capacity. Teams found creative ways to batch updates, implement efficient caching strategies, and minimize database queries. Many implemented custom PubSub patterns to reduce broadcast overhead for frequently changing data.

Documentation and knowledge sharing emerged as crucial factors for long term maintenance. Teams that invested in keeping their documentation current and accessible found it easier to onboard new team members and maintain system reliability. Many adopted automated documentation generation tools and maintained living architecture documents that evolved with their systems.

These real world experiences demonstrate that successful scaling requires a combination of technical solutions and organizational practices. Teams that planned for scale from the beginning while maintaining flexibility to adapt to changing requirements were most successful. Regular review and refinement of scaling strategies helped ensure systems could grow while maintaining performance and reliability.

The lessons learned from these case studies continue to inform best practices in building and scaling real time Phoenix applications. They demonstrate that while scaling presents significant challenges, careful planning and iterative improvement can lead to robust and maintainable systems serving millions of users.

## About the Publisher

**Northwood Lore Books** is an independent imprint dedicated to producing accessible, thought-provoking content through the use of advanced content generation systems. All books published under this imprint are created for educational or entertainment purposes only. Authors listed under this imprint use pen names and are not subject-matter experts. Accordingly, no material should be interpreted as financial, legal, medical, or professional advice. The information provided is general in nature, subject to change, and may not reflect the most current data or guidance. Readers are encouraged to consult official sources or qualified professionals before making decisions based on the content herein.

www.ingramcontent.com/pod-product-compliance
Lightning Source LLC
LaVergne TN
LVHW052252200926
848481LV00002B/344